Instructor's Manual

to accompany

Contemporary Labor Economics

Fifth Edition

Campbell R. McConnell

University of Nebraska-Lincoln

Stanley L. Brue

Pacific Lutheran University

David A. Macpherson

Florida State University

Prepared by

Norris Peterson
Pacific Lutheran University

McGraw-Hill College

Boston   Burr Ridge, IL   Dubuque, IA   Madison, WI   New York   San Francisco   St. Louis
Bangkok   Bogotá   Caracas   Lisbon   London   Madrid
Mexico City   Milan   New Delhi   Seoul   Singapore   Sydney   Taipei   Toronto

McGraw-Hill College

A Division of The McGraw·Hill Companies

Instructor's Manual to accompany
CONTEMPORARY LABOR ECONOMICS

1 2 3 4 5 6 7 8 9 0 QPD/QPD 9 0 9 8

ISBN 0-07-046041-8

www.mhhe.com

CONTENTS

NOTE TO INSTRUCTORS

This *Instructor's Manual* contains several features to aid you and your students. These include:

1. Chapter Outlines: Each chapter begins with a comprehensive outline which follows the headings and subheadings of the text.

2. Learning Objectives: There is a list of objectives to guide the students' progress through each chapter.

3. Answers to selected end-of-chapter text questions: While many of the end-of-chapter text questions are subjective, some require numerical answers or a straightforward objective response. The *Instructor's Manual* provides answers to some of the latter, as well as to a few of the subjective questions which have a particular "twist" to them.

4. Multiple-choice questions: There are almost 700 multiple-choice questions included in the *Manual*. While many are new, a substantial number were imported with slight revision from the now-discontinued *Student Workbook*. All are derived directly from the text and are suitable for constructing objective examinations.

5. Sample problems and essay questions: There are almost 60 open-ended questions suitable for use on examinations. Many of the questions incorporate material from two or more chapters.

CHAPTER 1
Labor Economics: Introduction and Overview

I.   LABOR ECONOMICS AS A DISCIPLINE
    A.   Socioeconomic Issues
    B.   Quantitative Importance
    C.   Unique Characteristics

II. THE "OLD" AND THE "NEW"

III. ECONOMIC PERSPECTIVE
    A.   Relative Scarcity
    B.   Purposeful Behavior
    C.   Adaptability

IV. OVERVIEW

V.   PAYOFFS
    A.   Personal Perspective
    B.   Social Perspective

WORLD OF WORK
    1.   Gary Becker: Nobel Laureate
    2.   Lotto Winners: Who Quit?

LEARNING OBJECTIVES

After learning the material in Chapter 1 of *Contemporary Labor Economics*, the student should be able to:

1.   explain why labor economics is justified as a special field of inquiry

2.   describe how the economic perspective can be applied to analysis of labor markets

3.   list and explain the basic assumptions underlying the choice-theoretic approach to labor economics

4.   identify those topics in labor economics that are mainly "microeconomic" and those that are primarily "macroeconomic"

5.   describe several benefits that derive from understanding labor economics

ANSWERS TO SELECTED END-OF-CHAPTER QUESTIONS

3.   Statements (a) and (c) pertain to macroeconomics; (b), (d), and (e) pertain to microeconomics.

6.   The "old" labor economics focused on descriptive and historical accounts of labor markets and related institutions. The "new" labor economics uses the economic perspective—relative scarcity, purposeful behavior, and adaptability—to describe the operation of labor markets.

MULTIPLE CHOICE QUESTIONS

1. Because resources are scarce relative to human wants, economics is best described as:
   a. the science of allocating productive resources fairly
   b.* a science of choice
   c. the science of allocating goods and services fairly
   d. the set of natural laws that govern human behavior in the face of adverse conditions

2. Labor economics is studied as a distinct subfield of economics because:
   a. the bulk of national income is received by labor
   b. the concepts of supply and demand must be revised somewhat when applied to labor markets
   c. labor economics can be used to analyze major socioeconomic trends such as the surge in the number of women workers
   d.* all of the above

3. The concept of demand must be modified when applied to labor markets to reflect the fact that:
   a. non-monetary characteristics of jobs may be as important to workers as their pay
   b. labor demand curves slope upward from left to right
   c.* the demand for labor is derived from the demand for the various products that labor produces
   d. the demand for output is derived from the demand for labor used to produce that output

4. The "old" view of labor economics stresses _____ while the "new" view focuses upon _____.
   a. analysis; markets
   b.* description; analysis
   c. description; institutions
   d. institutions; description

5. Because scarcity forces people to make purposeful choices, labor market participants:
   a. work as many hours as possible
   b.* respond to changes in perceived costs and benefits
   c. make choices that cannot be predicted
   d. must have perfect information

6. Which one of the following topics is most suited to macroeconomic analysis?
   a. Labor supply decisions of married women
   b. Short-run labor demand in a particular industry
   c. The individual decision on how much education to obtain
   d.* The impact of a recession on the country's unemployment rate

7. (*World of Work* 1-1) Nobel Laureate Gary Becker is known for economic theories in all of the following areas *except*:
   a. economics of households
   b. investment in human capital
   c.* the "old" labor economics
   d. economics of discrimination

8. (*World of Work* 1-2) According to a newspaper account from Washington State, lottery winners in that state:
   a.* usually continued to work when prizes were $1 million or less and usually quit work when prizes exceeded $4 million
   b. usually continued to work, no matter how large the prize
   c. usually quit work, no matter how large the prize
   d. were less likely to quit work the larger was the prize

CHAPTER 2
The Theory of Individual Labor Supply

I. THE WORK-LEISURE DECISION: BASIC MODEL
    A.   Indifference Curves
        1.   Negative Slope
        2.   Convex to Origin
        3.   Indifference Map
        4.   Different Work-Leisure Preferences
    B.   Budget Constraint
    C.   Utility Maximization
    D.   Wage Rate Changes: Income and Substitution Effects
        1.   Income Effect
        2.   Substitution Effect
        3.   Net Effect
    E.   Graphic Portrayal of Income and Substitution Effects
    F.   Rationale for Backward-Bending Supply Curve
    G.   Empirical Evidence
    H.   Elasticity versus Changes in Labor Supply

II. APPLYING AND EXTENDING THE MODEL
    A.   Nonparticipants and the Reservation Wage
    B.   Standard Workday
        1.   Overemployment
        2.   Underemployment
    C.   Premium Pay versus Straight Time
    D.   Income Maintenance Programs
        1.   Three Basic Features
            a.   The Income Guarantee or Basic Benefit, B
            b.   The Benefit-Reduction Rate, t
            c.   The Break-Even Level of Income, Y_b
        2.   Illustration
        3.   Controversy
        4.   Experimental Evidence

WORLD OF WORK
    1.   Sleep Time linked to Earnings
    2.   The Carnegie Conjecture
    3.   Moonlighting is on the Rise
    4.   The End of Welfare as an Entitlement

GLOBAL PERSPECTIVE
    1.   Annual Hours of Work per Employee, 1995

LEARNING OBJECTIVES

After learning the material in Chapter 2 of *Contemporary Labor Economics*, the student should be able to:

1. graph an indifference map for a person who values leisure and income

2. explain how the slope of the indifference curve relates to the marginal rate of substitution of leisure for income

3. explain why there is a diminishing marginal rate of substitution of leisure for income, which results in convex indifference curves

4. explain why indifference curves farther from the origin represent higher levels of utility

5. describe how personal differences in work-leisure preferences lead to differences in the shapes of indifference curves among individuals

6. graph a budget constraint and explain how its slope relates to the wage rate

7. identify, using the basic income-leisure model, the combination of income and leisure that maximizes a person's utility

8. distinguish between the income effect and substitution effect and isolate each on a graph

9. explain, in terms of income and substitution effects, why the typical labor supply curve for an individual slopes upward and to the right at relatively low wage rates and then bends backward and to the left at relatively high wage rates

10. explain the concept of wage elasticity of labor supply

11. explain why a person with non-labor income may choose not to participate in the labor force, relating this decision to the concept of the reservation wage

12. explain why a person may choose to "moonlight" or to work part-time

13. show in a graph how unpaid absenteeism may be related to requirements that people work a standard 40-hour week

14. show graphically that a person's utility-maximizing number of work hours may increase in response to a premium wage for overtime work

15. examine an income maintenance plan and determine the basic benefit, the benefit-reduction rate, and the break-even level of income

16. show, using the income-leisure model, why an income maintenance plan may reduce incentives to work

ANSWERS TO SELECTED END-OF-CHAPTER QUESTIONS

3. More hours in (a) and (b); fewer hours in (c) and (d).

4. The outcome assumes the substitution effect is stronger than the income effect. The statement reflects empirical evidence that the substitution effect strongly dominates the income effect for females, but the income effect weakly dominates the substitution effect for males.

5. She will choose the high-wage option. She will feel underemployed, but this option will allow her to reach a higher indifference curve (a higher level of utility.)

11. The subsidy is $2400. The total income is $4400. The break-even level of income is $10,000.

12. HBW' entails a zero benefit-reduction rate and the weakest disincentives to work. In contrast, HBYW entails a 100% benefit-reduction rate and the strongest disincentives to work.

MULTIPLE CHOICE QUESTIONS

1. The convex shape of a standard indifference curve reflects:
   a.* a diminishing marginal rate of substitution of leisure for income
   b. an increasing marginal rate of substitution of leisure for income
   c. a constant marginal rate of substitution of leisure for income
   d. the wage rate

2. The shape of a standard budget constraint reflects:
   a. a diminishing marginal rate of substitution of leisure for income
   b. an increasing marginal rate of substitution of leisure for income
   c. a constant marginal rate of substitution of leisure for income
   d.* the wage rate

3. In an income-leisure diagram, the wage rate is graphically represented by the:
   a. slope of the indifference curves
   b. curvature of the indifference curves
   c.* slope of the budget line
   d. tangency of the budget line with an indifference curve

4. Indifference curves are convex to the origin because:
   a. at a lower income, a person is more willing to sacrifice income for additional leisure
   b.* at a lower income, a person is less willing to sacrifice income for additional leisure
   c. at any income level, a person is willing to sacrifice the same amount of income for additional leisure
   d. the marginal rate of substitution of leisure for income is negative

5. The slope of an indifference curve at any point reflects the:
   a.* willingness of a person to substitute leisure for income
   b. wage rate
   c. income effect
   d. substitution effect

6. For income and leisure time, a higher level of utility is achieved by moving to the _____ on an indifference _____.
   a. northeast; curve   c.* northeast; map
   b. southwest; curve   d. southwest; map

5

Questions 7 and 8 refer to the following diagram:

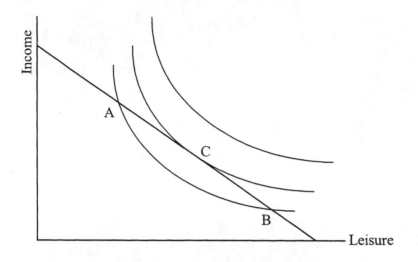

7.   Which of the following is a correct statement?
      a.   Position A is preferable to position B
      b.   Position A is preferable to position C
      c.   Position B is preferable to position C
      d.*   Position C is preferable to position A

8.   Which of the following is a correct statement?
      a.*   At A the individual's marginal valuation of leisure is higher than the market wage
      b.   At B the individual's marginal valuation of leisure is higher than the market wage
      c.   At C the individual's marginal valuation of leisure is lower than the market wage
      d.   At B the individual values leisure the same amount as at A

Questions 9 – 12 refer to the following diagram:

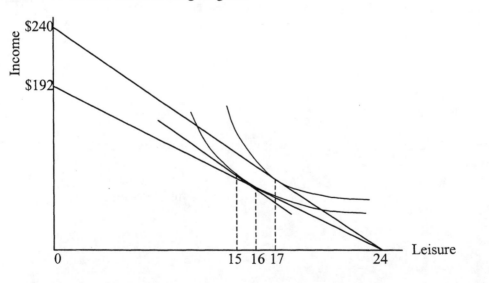

9.   If the person's optimal number of hours worked is seven hours, then the wage rate must be:
      a.* $10   c. $240
      b. $192   d.   cannot be determined

10.	The person has non-wage income of:
	a.*	$0	c.	$192
	b.	$10	d.	$240

11.	If this person's wage rate falls as illustrated in the diagram, then:
	a.	the substitution effect is stronger than the income effect
	b.*	the income effect is stronger than the substitution effect
	c.	this person's non-wage income will fall as well
	d.	the substitution effect causes desired work hours to increase

12.	The income effect of the illustrated wage decrease causes this individual to work:
	a.	one less hour	c.	two less hours
	b.	one more hour	d.*	two more hours

13.	The income effect is:
	a.	the combination of leisure and wage rate that maximizes one's income
	b.*	that part of the total change in desired work hours that is due to the change in real income resulting from a change in the wage rate
	c.	that part of the total change in desired work hours that is due to a change in the wage rate, with real income or utility constant
	d.	always dominated by the substitution effect

14.	The substitution effect is:
	a.	the combination of leisure and wage rate that maximizes one's income
	b.	that part of the total change in desired work hours that is due to the change in real income resulting from a change in the wage rate
	c.*	that part of the total change in desired work hours that is due to a change in the wage rate, with real income or utility constant
	d.	always dominated by the income effect

15.	Which one of the following would be most likely to shift the labor supply curve to the right?
	a.	A decrease in the wage rate
	b.	A change in the indifference map following deterioration of working conditions
	c.*	A change in the indifference map following an improvement in working conditions
	d.	A significant increase in dividend and interest income

16.	Consider the impact of a general increase in real wages on both men and women. Empirical evidence suggests that men will tend to work _____ hour and women will tend to work _____ hours.
	a.	more; fewer	c.	fewer; fewer
	b.	more; more	d.*	fewer; more

17.	Which of the following would unambiguously predict a decrease in desired hours of work?
	a.*	The substitution effect of a wage decrease
	b.	The income effect of a wage increase
	c.	A wage increase
	d.	The substitution effect of a decline in income tax rates

Questions 18 – 20 are based on the following diagram, which shows a labor supply curve for an individual.

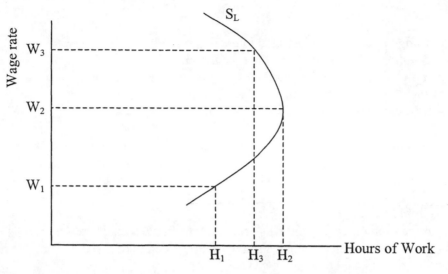

18. If the wage rises from W_1 to W_2 we may conclude that:
    a. the income effect is stronger than the substitution effect
    b. the income effect and substitution effects are equal
    c.* the substitution effect is stronger than the income effect
    d. labor supply is perfectly inelastic

19. If this person were now willing to supply H_1 hours of work at W_3, we could conclude that:
    a. labor supply increased (the curve shifted to the right)
    b.* labor supply decreased (the curve shifted to the left)
    c. the person's preferences did not change
    d. the substitution and income effects are now equal

20. Of the following, which one would most likely cause this person to supply H_1 hours of work at W_3 rather than the current H_3 hours?
    a.* An increase in income received by this person's spouse
    b. A decrease in this person's marginal valuation of leisure time
    c. Congress abolishes an income maintenance program
    d. A decrease in income received by this person's spouse

21. Suppose an individual worker is on the backward-bending portion of her labor supply curve. Then for a wage increase the:
    a. income and substitution effects both increase desired work hours
    b. income and substitution effects are equal
    c* income effect is stronger than the substitution effect
    d. substitution effect is stronger than the income effect

Questions 22 – 26 are based on the following diagram:

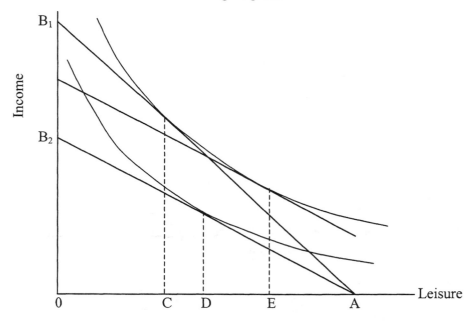

22.   If the current wage rate results in a budget constraint of AB_1, the individual will choose:
       a.   0C hours of work and AC hours of leisure
       b.   AD hours of work and 0D hours of leisure
       c.   0D hours of work and AD hours of leisure
       d.*   AC hours of work and 0C hours of leisure

23.   The shift from budget line AB_1 to AB_2 implies a:
       a.*   decrease in the wage rate   c.   increase in the wage rate
       b.   decrease in non-wage income   d.   increase in non-wage income

24.   The equilibrium positions shown imply that in the relevant wage range this person is:
       a.*   on the upsloping segment of the individual labor supply curve
       b.   on the backward-bending segment of the individual labor supply curve
       c.   at the point on the individual labor supply curve where the income and substitution
               effects are equal
       d.   being offered a wage less than the reservation wage

25.   The equilibrium positions shown in the diagram imply that for a wage increase:
       a.   both the income and substitution effects increase desired work hours
       b.   both the income and substitution effects reduce desired work hours
       c.   the income effect increases desired work hours and the substitution effect reduces desired
               work hours
       d.*   the income effect reduces desired work hours and the substitution effect increases desired
               work hours

26.   In the diagram, the substitution effect associated with a wage increase is shown by the distance:
       a.   CD   b.   DE   c.*   CE   d.   0C

9

27. Suppose an individual worker is on the upsloping portion of her labor supply curve. Then for a wage increase the:
   a. income and substitution effects both increase desired work hours
   b. income and substitution effects are equal
   c. income effect is stronger than the substitution effect
   d* substitution effect is stronger than the income effect

28. Which of the following circumstances will increase the likelihood of an individual being a non-participant in the labor market?
   a. High earnings capacity in the labor market
   b. The absence of non-wage income
   c. A potential market wage that exceeds the individual's reservation wage
   d* Availability of substantial non-wage income

29. Sammy is required by her employer to work a standard eight-hour workday. Suppose her marginal rate of substitution of leisure for income is less than the wage rate at this level of work effort. We can conclude that Sammy will:
   a* feel underemployed
   b. probably have a higher than average absenteeism rate
   c. feel overemployed
   d. prefer to work part-time, if such a job is available at the same wage rate

Questions 30 and 31 are based on the following diagram. TS represents the standard 40 hour work week. Indifference curves labeled with subscripts "a" and "b" are for individuals A and B, respectively.

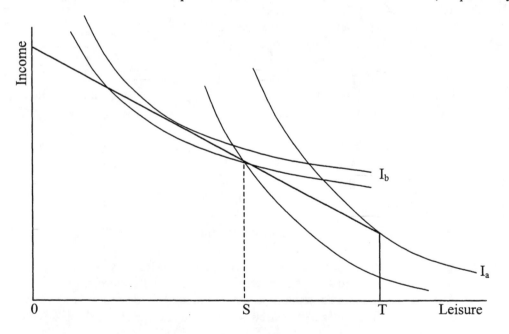

30. Assuming workers must work TS hours or not at all, worker A will:
   a* not participate in the labor force
   b. be at an optimum at TS hours of work
   c. work the standard work week but will feel overemployed
   d. work the standard work week but will feel underemployed

10

31. Assuming workers must work TS hours or not at all, worker B will:
    a.   not participate in the labor force
    b.   be at an optimum at TS hours of work
    c.   work the standard work week but will feel overemployed
    d*   work the standard work week but will feel underemployed

32. Compared to workers with less education, people who have more education tend to earn higher wages and have higher pensions upon retirement. Given this observation, which of the following statements best explains why those persons with more education also retire at a later age?
    a.   If tastes for leisure are the same, the effect of the higher pension must outweigh the effects of the higher wages
    b*   If tastes for leisure are the same, the effects of the higher wages must outweigh the effects of the higher pensions
    c.   Since higher wages and pensions both suggest a lower retirement age, those with more education must value leisure less
    d.   Regardless of the tastes for leisure, the higher wages and pensions would both suggest a higher retirement age

Questions 33 and 34 refer to the following diagram:

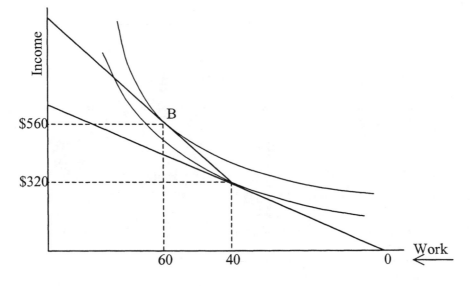

33. Suppose this worker is currently working 40 hours per week and earning $8 per hour. Which one of the following would cause a move to point B, and the subsequent increase in work hours to 60?
    a*   The availability of overtime work at $12 per hour
    b.   The availability of a moonlighting job that pays $6 per hour
    c.   An increase in the straight-time wage to $9.33 per hour
    d.   An increase in non-wage income of $240

34. Suppose this worker's union negotiates an increase in the straight-time wage from $8 to $9.33 per hour with no bonus for overtime. This plan would allow earnings of $560 at 60 hours per week. Assuming this worker can freely choose the number of hours worked, he will choose to work:
    a.   60 hours per week
    b*   fewer than 60 hours per week
    c.   more than 60 hours per week
    d.   more than 60 hours per week if the income effect dominates; less otherwise

Questions 35 and 36 are based on the following information: Assume under an income maintenance program that the basic benefit (income guarantee) is $9000 and the benefit-reduction rate is 50%.

35.　　If a family has an earned income of $3000 per year, its subsidy payment will be:
　　　　a.　　$6000　　b.*　　$7500　　c.　　$9000　　d.　　$0

36.　　The break-even level of income is:
　　　　a.　　$4500　　b.　　$6000　　c.　　$9000　　d.*　　$18,000

37.　　Suppose an income maintenance program offers a basic benefit of $7500 per year and the benefit-reduction rate is 33 1/3%. The break-even level of income is then:
　　　　a.　　$2500　　b.　　$7500　　c.　　$15,000　　d.*　　$22,500

38.　　(*World of Work* 2-1) A study by Biddle and Hamermesh found that increasing wages:
　　　　a.*　　reduced sleep time for men but not for women
　　　　b.　　caused both men and women to substitute "waking leisure" for sleep time
　　　　c.　　had no impact on sleep time
　　　　d.　　reduced sleep time for women but not for men

39.　　(*World of Work* 2-2) Empirical evidence indicates that inheritances _____ labor force participation; further, persons receiving inheritances tended to be _____ likely to work in the years preceding the inheritance.
　　　　a.　　have no impact on; less　　　　c.　　reduce; equally
　　　　b.　　reduce; more　　　　　　　　d.*　　reduce; less

40.　　(*World of Work* 2-3) The percentage of the labor force holding two or more jobs was _____ in 1995 compared to 1975.
　　　　a.　　lower　　b.　　the same　　c.*　　higher　　d.　　twice as high

41.　　(*World of Work* 2-4) The Personal Responsibility and Work Opportunity Act of 1996:
　　　　a.　　moved control over welfare spending from states to the federal government
　　　　b.　　removed lifetime limits on welfare eligibility
　　　　c*　　with few exceptions, requires welfare recipients to work after two years of receiving assistance
　　　　d.　　provided welfare benefits to qualified immigrants

CHAPTER 3
Population, Participation Rates, and Hours of Work

I.   THE POPULATION BASE

II.   BECKER'S MODEL: THE ALLOCATION OF TIME
    A.   Two Fundamental Changes
          1.   Household Perspective
          2.   Multiple Uses of Time
    B.   Commodity Characteristics
    C.   Household Choices
    D.   Income and Substitution Effects Revisited

III. PARTICIPATION RATES: DEFINED AND MEASURED

IV.   SECULAR TREND OF PARTICIPATION RATES
    A.   Declining Participation Rates of Older Males
          1.   Rising Real Wages and Earnings
          2.   Social Security and Private Pensions
          3.   Disability Benefits
          4.   Life-Cycle Considerations
    B.   Rising Female Participation Rates
          1.   Rising Real Wage Rates for Women
          2.   Changing Preferences and Attitudes
          3.   Rising Productivity in the Household
          4.   Declining Birthrates
          5.   Rising Divorce Rates
          6.   Expanding Job Accessibility
          7.   Attempts to Maintain Living Standards
    C.   Relative Importance
    D.   Racial Differences
          1.   Females
          2.   Males

V.   CYCLICAL CHANGES IN PARTICIPATION RATES
    A.   Added-Worker Effect
    B.   Discouraged-Worker Effect
    C.   Procyclical Labor Force Changes

VI.   HOURS OF WORK: TWO TRENDS
    A.   Workweek Decline, 1900 – 1940
    B.   Post-World War II: Workweek Stability
          1.   FLSA
          2.   Higher Tax Rates
          3.   Education
          4.   Advertising
          5.   "Catching up"

WORLD OF WORK
1. The Changing Face of America
2. Working for Free
3. Does Technological Change Induce Early Retirement ?
4. Economics and Fertility
5. Family and Medical Leave Act of 1993

GLOBAL PERSPECTIVE
1. Men's and Women's Hours of Home Work, 1995
2. Labor Force Participation of Women Aged 25 – 54, 1995
3. Maximum Duration of Statutory Leave in Weeks

LEARNING OBJECTIVES

After learning the material in Chapter 3 of *Contemporary Labor Economics*, the student should be able to:

1. explain the importance of time in determining household consumption patterns

2. contrast the terms "commodity," "income effect," and "substitution effect" as used in Becker's model of the allocation of time with their counterparts from Chapter 2

3. describe the role of comparative advantage in the operation of households

4. compute the labor force participation rate and compare this rate across demographic groups in the population

5. describe changes in male and female labor force participation rates over the years and explain why these changes have occurred

6. describe changes in labor force participation rates among racial and ethnic groups over the years and explain why these changes have occurred

7. explain how life-cycle considerations may determine labor force participation

8. describe how the "added-worker effect" and the "discouraged-worker effect" influence labor force participation rates over the business cycle

9. cite the reasons for the workweek decline in the early twentieth century and the relative stability of the workweek since World War II

ANSWERS TO SELECTED END-OF-CHAPTER QUESTIONS

3. The labor force participation rate was 132 / (263 – 64) =66.3%.

4. The aggregate labor force participation rate has increased. The participation rate of males has decreased while that of females has increased.

9. See the diagram at right. A Black with these preferences and the heavier budget line would choose not to enter the labor force. A white with the same preferences but facing the lighter budget line would enter the labor force.

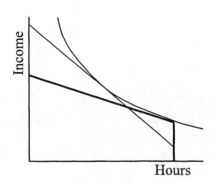

14

10. No. The discouraged-worker effect reduces labor force participation as the unemployment rate increases while the added-worker effect increases it. Empirical evidence suggests the discouraged-worker effect is dominant so that the labor force participation rate varies inversely with the unemployment rate.

11. Yes. The added-worker effect is based on a reduction in the partner's non-wage income. The discouraged-worker effect can be explained by a reduction in the expected wage rate (the potential wage adjusted for the reduced probability of finding a job.)

13. Higher taxes decrease the slope of the budget line. Advertising and attempts to maintain living standards may have changed preferences in favor of work so that more goods can be acquired.

MULTIPLE CHOICE QUESTIONS

1. In Becker's model of time allocation, the difference between "goods" and "commodities" is that commodities are produced:
   a. in markets while goods are produced in households
   b. only with housework
   c.* by combining goods with time
   d. in the market, while goods are produced in the home

2. If a worker's wage rate rises:
   a. time-intensive commodities will tend to be substituted for goods-intensive commodities in household production
   b.* goods-intensive commodities will tend to be substituted for time-intensive commodities in household production
   c. more leisure time will be consumed
   d. more leisure time will be consumed if the substitution effect outweighs the income effect

3. Compared to a high-wage worker, a low-wage worker will tend to:
   a. pursue more goods-intensive activities
   b.* pursue more time-intensive activities
   c. pursue fewer time-intensive activities
   d. sacrifice time-intensive activities in favor of goods-intensive activities

4. Which of the following best exemplifies the Becker substitution effect? An increase in wages leads a family to:
   a.* eat more meals at restaurants
   b. play more golf together
   c. have more children
   d. take fewer, but longer vacations

5. In a particular family, both spouse A and spouse B could earn $15 per hour in market work. However, spouse A has a comparative advantage in the production of home-produced goods. Becker's model of time allocation predicts that:
   a. spouse B will be better able to substitute time for goods in the production of commodities
   b. spouse A and spouse B will divide market work and home production equally
   c. spouse A will tend to specialize in market work; spouse B in home production
   d.* spouse A will tend to specialize in home production; spouse B in market work

6. The labor force consists of all persons aged 16 years and older who are:
   a. employed
   b.* employed or are actively seeking employment
   c. employed, actively seeking employment, or have given up looking for employment
   d. not institutionalized

7. The labor force participation rate:
   a. is the fraction of a given population that is classified as employed
   b. has been rising for males and declining for females
   c. tends to increase during a recession, due to the combined added-worker effect and discouraged-worker effect
   d.* is the fraction of a given population that is classified either as employed or unemployed

8. Given the following data, what is the labor force participation rate?

Population	250 million
Non-institutionalized population, age 16 and over	200 million
Persons employed or seeking employment	150 million
Unemployed persons	20 million

   a. 10%   b.* 75%   c. 80%   d. 87%

9. The unemployment rate measures the proportion of the:
   a. civilian population that is classified as unemployed
   b. civilian population that is not in the labor force
   c. labor force that did not report to work during the survey week
   d.* labor force that is classified as unemployed

10.
Males in the labor force	100 million
Unemployed males	5 million
Non-institutionalized females, age 16 and over	110 million
Employed or unemployed females	88 million

    Considering the information in the table, the male labor force participation rate _____ and the female labor force participation rate _____.
    a. is 95%; is 80%
    b. is 95%; is 88%
    c.* cannot be calculated from the data; is 80%
    d. cannot be calculated from the data; cannot be calculated from the data

11. The aggregate labor force participation rate in the U. S. is currently about:
    a. one-fourth   c.* two-thirds
    b. one-half   d. three-fourths

12. Since 1970, the labor force participation rate of women has _____ and the participation rate of men has _____, so the aggregate participation rate has _____.
    a. risen; been unchanged; risen   c. fallen; risen; increased slightly
    b.* risen; fallen; increased slightly   d. risen; fallen; fallen

13. Since 1970, the labor force participation rate of 25 – 54 year-old men has _____, the participation rate of 55 – 64 year-old men has _____, and the participation rate of men age 65 and over has _____.

   a.   risen; been steady; risen   c.   risen; fallen; been steady
   b.   fallen; risen; risen   d.*   been steady; fallen; fallen

14. Which one of the following is *not* a plausible explanation of the observed change in the participation rate of males age 65 and older since World War II?
   a.   The increasing practice of granting pension benefits at earlier ages
   b.*   Cutbacks in Social Security benefits
   c.   The long-term growth of average real incomes and wealth
   d.   The increased generosity of the disability component of Social Security

✓ 15. Which one of the following gives rise to a retirement-inducing substitution effect? As workers approach retirement age:
   a.   Social Security benefits become available
   b.   wealth becomes sufficient to make retirement affordable
   c.   earnings potential decreases and leisure becomes relatively more costly
   d.*   earnings potential decreases and leisure becomes relatively less costly

16. Which one of the following is *not* predicted to increase the labor force participation rate of married women?
   a.*   Rising wage rates for husbands
   b.   Rising productivity in the household
   c.   Declining birthrates
   d.   Attempts to maintain living standards

17. "For married women, the substitution effect of rising wage rates has apparently outweighed the income effect." This statement is:
   a.*   true because the labor force participation rate of women has been increasing
   b   true because married women have had to work to maintain household living standards
   c.   not true because the labor force participation rate of women has been increasing
   d.   not true because the labor force participation rate of women has been declining

18. According to the textbook, each of the following factors may have contributed to increased female labor force participation *except*:
   a.   rising divorce rates
   b.   expanding job accessibility
   c.*   fewer educational opportunities
   d.   a desire to maintain household living standards

19. The secular decline in the birth rate:
   a.   has contributed to the increased labor force participation rate of women
   b.   may partly be caused by the increasing opportunity cost of children as women's wages have increased
   c.*   both a. and b. are correct
   d.   neither a. nor b. are correct

20. Fuchs' research suggests the most important reasons for the increased labor force participation rate of women are:
    a.* rising real wages and expansion of service sector jobs
    b. rising real wages and the feminist movement
    c. the feminist movement and passage of antidiscrimination legislation
    d. passage of antidiscrimination legislation and technological innovations in household production methods

21. Compared to white females, the labor force participation rate of black females is _____.
    Compared to white males the labor force participation rate of black males is _____.
    a. nearly identical; the same   c. lower; greater
    b. greater; lower   d.* nearly identical; lower

22. In the mid-1950s, white males:
    a. were more likely to participate in the labor force than were black males
    b. were less likely to participate in the labor force than were black males
    c. and black males were about equally likely to participate in the labor force and that relationship still holds
    d.* and black males were about equally likely to participate in the labor force but now white men have a higher participation rate

23. The labor force participation rate of white women has:
    a.* increased until it nearly equals that of black women
    b. fallen until it nearly equals that of black women
    c. increased and now significantly exceeds that of black women
    d. been steady since World War II

24. Until recently, the labor force participation rate of black women has _____ the rate of white women. In recent years the labor force participation rate of black men has _____ the rate of white men.
    a. been slightly less than; consistently exceeded
    b.* consistently exceeded; been slightly less than
    c. consistently exceeded; consistently exceeded
    d. been slightly less than; been slightly less than

25. A "supply side" explanation of the lower participation rate of black males compared to white males is that:
    a. blacks command lower wage rates and are usually last-hired and first-fired
    b. black workers are located in the inner city while jobs are in the suburbs
    c. black women's labor force participation rate is lower than that of white women
    d.* opportunities outside the labor market, such as social security and public assistance, afford comparatively more attractive alternatives to blacks

26. Which one of the following will tend to increase the likelihood of participation in the labor force for a current non-participant?
    a.* A decrease in the spouse's wage
    b. An increase in the spouse's wage
    c. An increase in family size
    d. Falling productivity in household production of commodities

27. Which one of the following statements is correct?
 a. The added-worker effect and the discouraged-worker effect tend to operate in the same direction
 b.* The added-worker effect and the discouraged-worker effect tend to operate in different directions
 c. The added-worker effect is relatively strong as the economy expands and wages rise
 d. The discouraged-worker effect is relatively strong as the economy expands and wages rise

28. The added-worker effect suggests that:
 a. higher wages will attract more persons into the labor market during market expansions
 b.* when one family member loses a job, other family members may enter the labor force
 c. the measured unemployment rate probably understates the true economic hardship associated with unemployment
 d. the labor force participation rate will fall as the unemployment rate rises

29. Because of the _____, the unemployment rate as measured by the Bureau of Labor Statistics tends to understate the extent of unemployment during a recession.
 a. labor force participation rate
 b. added-worker effect
 c. decline in the average workweek
 d.* discouraged-worker effect

30. The discouraged-worker effect indicates that:
 a. married women will enter the labor force to maintain household living standards after their husbands' wages have fallen
 b. some unemployed persons in the labor force actively seek employment
 c.* some unemployed workers will decide to withdraw from the labor force as the unemployment rate increases
 d. the labor force participation rate varies directly with the unemployment rate

31. Since the end of World War II, the average weekly hours of work in manufacturing has
 a.* been steady, in part due to "catching up"
 b. been steady, in part due to lower tax rates
 c. fallen sharply
 d. increased sharply

32. (*World of Work* 3-1) According to "The Changing Face of America:"
 a. immigration will not significantly affect the U. S. population between the 1990s and the year 2050
 b. the ratio of paid workers to Social Security recipients will fall dramatically
 c. the projected slowdown in labor force growth will last until the middle of the 21st century
 d.* the projected slowdown in labor force growth will be only temporary

33. (*World of Work* 3-2) Freeman's research on volunteers finds that:
 a. volunteers are concentrated among those with a low opportunity cost of time
 b. volunteering accounts for over 10% of total work time
 c. being asked to volunteer has little impact on the number of hours volunteered
 d.* high income individuals tend to substitute monetary gifts for donations of time

34.   (*World of Work* 3-3) Research by Ann P. Bartel and Nachum Sicherman finds evidence that:
    a.   workers retire earlier in industries with high continuous rates of technological change
    b.   unexpected changes in technology lead older workers to retire later
    c.*   unexpected changes in technology lead older workers to retire earlier
    d.   retirement behavior is not at all related to technological changes

35.   (*World of Work* 3-4) In examining factors affecting fertility, researchers have observed that:
    a.   higher income families tend to have more children than lower income families
    b.*   lower income families tend to have more children than higher income families
    c.   birthrates are unrelated to household incomes
    d.   income effects of higher wages influence birth rates but not substitution effects

36.   (*World of Work* 3-5) The Family and Medical Leave Act of 1993:
    a.   applies equally to large and small firms
    b.   guarantees workers paid leave for family and medical emergencies
    c.   applies to both full-time and part-time workers
    d.*   does not necessarily apply to the highest-paid ten percent of workers at covered firms

CHAPTER 4
Labor Quality: Investing in Human Capital

I.   INVESTMENT IN HUMAN CAPITAL: CONCEPT AND DATA

II.   THE HUMAN CAPITAL MODEL
- A.   Discounting and Net Present Value
  - 1.   Time Preference
  - 2.   Present Value Formula
  - 3.   Decision Rule: $V_p > 0$
  - 4.   Illustration
- B.   Internal Rate of Return
  - 1.   Formula
  - 2.   Decision Rule: $r = i$
- C.   Generalizations and Implications
  - 1.   Length of Income Stream
  - 2.   Costs
  - 3.   Earnings Differentials
- D.   Empirical Data
  - 1.   Rate-of-return Studies
  - 2.   The College Wage Premium
  - 3.   Caveats
  - 4.   Private versus Social Perspective

III.   HUMAN CAPITAL INVESTMENT AND THE DISTRIBUTION OF EARNINGS
- A.   Diminishing Rates of Return
  - 1.   Diminishing Returns
  - 2.   Falling Benefits, Rising Costs
- B.   Demand, Supply, and Equilibrium
- C.   Differences in Human Capital Investment
  - 1.   Ability Differences
  - 2.   Discrimination: Uncertainty of Earnings
  - 3.   Access to Funds
  - 4.   Interactions
- D.   Capital Market Imperfections

IV.   ON-THE-JOB TRAINING
- A.   Costs and Benefits
- B.   General and Specific Training
- C.   Distributing Training costs
  - 1.   General Training
  - 2.   Specific Training
- D.   Modifications
- E.   Increasing Importance and Empirical Evidence

V.   CRITICISMS OF HUMAN CAPITAL THEORY
- A.   Investment or Consumption?
- B.   Non-wage Benefits

C. The Ability Problem
D. The Screening Hypothesis
E. Recapitulation

WORLD OF WORK
1. Twins, Education, and Earnings
2. Higher Education: Making the Right Choices
3. Job Training: Lessons from Germany?
4. The Radical Critique of Human Capital Theory

GLOBAL PERSPECTIVE
1. Hours Per Week Spent Studying Among High School Seniors
2. Schooling Quality

LEARNING OBJECTIVES

After learning the material in Chapter 4 of *Contemporary Labor Economics*, the student should be able to:

1. describe trends in age-earnings profiles

2. identify and graphically depict the costs and benefits of investing in human capital

3. compute the net present value of an income stream

4. explain the difference between net present value and the internal rate of return on an investment

5. describe the conditions required for optimal investment in human capital

6. summarize and critically evaluate the findings of empirical rate of return studies, especially recent trends in the college wage premium

7. distinguish between private and social benefits and costs of human capital investment

8. list the factors that lead to differences in human capital investment

9. explain why the demand for human capital curve is downward-sloping and cite factors that may shift the curve

10. distinguish between general and specific training, describing their effects on the investment decision and worker retention

11. explain why workers bear general training costs

12. explain why specific training leads an employer and a worker to establish a long-term relationship with each other

ANSWERS TO SELECTED END-OF-CHAPTER QUESTIONS

3. It is economically rational to enroll in the course. The net present value is $-(8000 + 1000) + 5000/1.1 + 5000/(1.1)^2 + 5000/(1.1)^3 = \$3,434.26$.

5. The college wage premium is the ratio of earnings for college graduates to the earnings of high school graduates. In the 1970s there was a large flow of new college graduates into the labor force that depressed the college wage premium. In the 1980s and '90s, the demand for college-trained workers increased and the college wage premium increased.

9. Scholarships based on ability will likely increase the dispersion of earnings to the extent that ability and schooling are positively correlated. Scholarships based on need are likely to reduce dispersion to the extent that parental income and schooling are negatively corrclated.

13. a. The private rate of return will not be biased, but the social rate of return will have an upward bias
   b. Upward bias
   c. Upward bias
   d. Downward bias

MULTIPLE CHOICE QUESTIONS

1. Available evidence indicates that:
   a. age-earnings profiles vary with education, but not with age
   b. age-earnings profiles vary with age, but not with education
   c. age-earnings profiles of workers with more education tend to be flatter, but higher, than those with less education
   d.* differences in earnings between workers who have more education and those who have less education generally widen with age

2. The total cost of formal education typically does *not* include:
   a. expenditures for tuition, books, and fees
   b. earnings foregone by choosing not to enter the labor force
   c.* expenditures for room and board
   d. transportation expenses to and from college

Questions 3 – 6 are based on the following diagram:

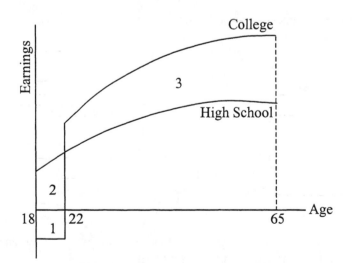

3. According to human capital theory, areas 1, 2, and 3 represent respectively:
   a. indirect costs, direct costs, and incremental earnings
   b.* direct costs, indirect costs, and incremental earnings
   c. indirect costs, direct costs, and total earnings
   d. direct costs, indirect costs, and total earnings

4. In deciding whether or not to go to college, one would compare the discounted value of:
   a. area 3 to the discounted value of areas 1
   b. area 3 to the discounted value of area 2
   c.* area 3 to the discounted value of areas 1 and 2
   d. areas 2 and 3 to the discounted value of area 1

5. Which one of the following would increase the likelihood of investing in a college education?
   a. an increase in area 1
   b.* a reduction in area 2
   c. a reduction in the retirement age
   d. a reduction in area 3 and an equal increase in area 2

6. Suppose there is now a 25% likelihood that a person's work career may be interrupted for ten years after schooling has been completed. In the diagram above, this development would:
   a. have no impact   c. shrink area 2
   b. shrink area 1   d.* shrink area 3

7. Consider an individual who will invest a total of $10,000 in direct and indirect costs for training in order to increase earnings by $12,500 for the next year. Suppose the interest rate is 8%. If this person plans to retire the following year, the net present value of this investment is:
   a. zero   c. $2500
   b.* between $1500 and $2500   d. between $11,500 and $12,500

8. An earnings maximizing student would attend college if:
   a. the net present value of a college education is zero
   b. the internal rate of return on a college education is positive
   c.* the internal rate of return on a college education exceeds the interest rate
   d. there is an earnings gain associated with a college education

9. At the optimal amount of education, the internal rate of return on education is:
   a. maximized
   b. higher than the market rate of interest
   c. lower than the market rate of interest
   d.* equal to the market rate of interest

10. Which one of the following circumstances would lead to increased investment in education by women?
    a. An increase in the likelihood of interrupted labor market careers
    b.* Employment opportunities for women improve
    c. Higher discount rates for women than men
    d. Persistent discrimination against women

11. Human capital theory predicts that the proportion of people attending college will decrease if:
    a.* the age at which retirement benefits are received is lowered to 59
    b. the age at which retirement benefits are received is raised to 75
    c. there is a relatively large population of new high school graduates
    d. the earnings of college graduates are reduced because of a large influx of highly-educated "baby boomers" into the workforce

12. Most rate-of-return studies of education indicate that:
    a.   social rates of return generally exceed private rates of return
    b.   private rates of return are about 2.5% – 7%
    c.* private rates of return are about 8% – 13%
    d.   private rates of return have been steady over the 1956 – 1995 period

13. The private rate of return on human capital may _____ the social rate because _____.
    a.   understate; schooling is subsidized
    b.* understate; schooling provides external benefits
    c.   overstate; schooling provides external benefits
    d.   overstate; schooling and ability are positively correlated

14. In calculating the social rate of return on a human capital investment one would:
    a.   deduct taxes from incremental earnings
    b.* treat public subsidies to education as a part of the costs
    c.   exclude any external benefits associated with the investment
    d.   treat public subsidies to training as part of the benefits

15. From 1980 to the present, the college wage premium
    a.   increased for women but fell for men
    b.   increased for men but fell for women
    c.   fell for both women and men
    d.* increased for both women and men

16. The increase in the college wage premium during the 1980s was most likely caused by:
    a.* increased demand for college graduates due to changes in the structure of the economy
    b.   increased supply of college graduates from the large "baby boom" generation
    c.   changes in technology that reduced the relative supply of college-trained workers
    d.   increased demand for high school graduates, particularly males

17. The declining college wage premium in the 1970s is generally attributed to:
    a.   growing demand for college graduates in that period
    b.   shrinking supply of college graduates in that period
    c.* growing supply of college graduates in that period
    d.   the shift of employment from manufacturing to services

18. Private loans to finance investments in human capital:
    a.   are difficult to obtain because the financial return to education has been decreasing in recent years
    b.* are difficult to obtain because a person cannot readily pledge collateral on human capital
    c.   are granted by banks just like to finance investment in machinery or houses, without regard to collateral
    d.   are rarely subsidized by government because they are granted readily by private banks

19. The demand for human capital curves slope downward and to the right because:
    a.   education is a screening device
    b.   as the interest rate rises, the net present value of education rises
    c.* the benefits of increased education diminish as schooling continues
    d.   investment in education is subject to increasing marginal returns

Questions 20 – 23 are based on the following diagram.

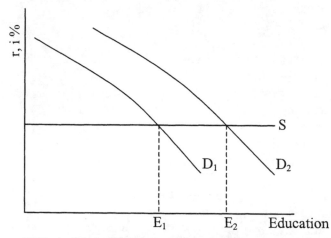

20.   If D_1 is this individual's investment demand curve, then the optimal amount of education:
       a.   is E_1 from society's standpoint
       b.   is E_2 from society's standpoint
       c.*   is E_1 from this individual's standpoint
       d.   cannot be determined without further information

21.   Which one of the following might cause a person's human capital investment demand curve to shift from D_1 to D_2?
       a.   The person discounts future earnings at a higher rate than before
       b.   The indirect costs of education increase
       c.   The college wage premium falls
       d.*   The college wage premium increases

22.   Compared to D_1, a person whose demand curve is given by D_2 will likely obtain:
       a.*   more education and receive higher earnings
       b.   more education and receive lower earnings
       c.   less education and receive higher earnings
       d.   less education and receive lower earnings

23.   Which one of the following will shift the supply curve downward?
       a.   A reduction in the availability of student loans
       b.   Greater ability to transform schooling into earnings
       c.   An increase in expected work life
       d.*   An increase in grants and scholarships

24.   Which one of the following most closely approximates pure specific training?
       a.   Learning tax accounting
       b.*   Learning a management information system that is unique to your firm
       c.   Majoring in management information systems at a major university
       d.   Learning a widely-used spreadsheet program that is used at your firm

25.   General training:
       a.*   will be paid for by the employee in the form of a reduced wage
       b.   raises the trainee's value only to the firm that is providing the training
       c.   helps to make labor a quasi-fixed resource
       d.   reduces the worker's value to the firm, because the worker's wage rate would have to rise

26. Specific training:
    a.   will be paid for by the employee in the form of a reduced wage
    b.   occurs once a student majors in a specific subject area
    c.*   helps to make labor a quasi-fixed resource
    d.   reduces the worker's value to the firm, because the worker's wage rate would have to rise

27. A worker who has obtained specific training is:
    a.   more likely to establish a long-term association with an employer because the worker has made an investment he does not wish to lose
    b.   more likely to establish a long-term association with an employer because the employer has made an investment she does not wish to lose
    c.*   both a. and b. are correct
    d.   neither a. nor b. is correct

28. Charley's employer is considering him for a training program that will cost $3 per hour. His current marginal revenue product is $15 per hour and will rise to $20 upon completion of the program. If this is *general* training, Charley's training and post-training wage, respectively, will most likely be:
    a. $15; $20   c. $12; $15
    b. $15; $17   d.* $12; $20

29. Mary's employer is considering her for a training program that will cost $3 per hour. Her current marginal revenue product is $15 per hour and will rise to $20 upon completion of the program. If this is *firm-specific* training, Mary's training and post-training wage, respectively, will most likely be:
    a. $15; $20   c. $12; $15
    b.* $15; $17   d. $12; $20

Questions 30 and 31 refer to the following diagram, in which MRP_u refers to the marginal revenue product of an untrained worker, while MRP_t refers to this worker's marginal revenue product as a result of a program of on-the-job training.

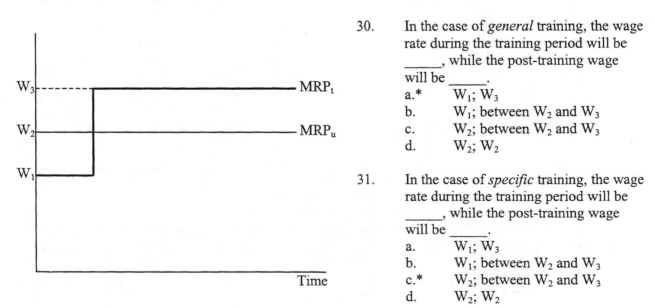

30. In the case of *general* training, the wage rate during the training period will be _____, while the post-training wage will be _____.
    a.* W_1; W_3
    b. W_1; between W_2 and W_3
    c. W_2; between W_2 and W_3
    d. W_2; W_2

31. In the case of *specific* training, the wage rate during the training period will be _____, while the post-training wage will be _____.
    a. W_1; W_3
    b. W_1; between W_2 and W_3
    c.* W_2; between W_2 and W_3
    d. W_2; W_2

32. Which of the following statements about on-the-job training is most supported by empirical evidence?
   a. A greater percentage of men receives job training than women
   b. Job training is more common at smaller firms than larger ones
   c.* Workers with more formal education also tend to receive more on-the-job training
   d. Training does not lead to higher job performance ratings

33. If the screening hypothesis is true:
   a. educational attainment and the level of fringe benefits received will be inversely related
   b.* the private rate of return to education will tend to overstate the social rate of return
   c. the private rate of return to education will not accurately reflect the gain to the individual student
   d. the college wage premium is much greater than is hypothesized by human capital theorists

34. (*World of Work* 4-1) Research by Ashenfelter and Krueger on educational attainment and earnings showed that:
   a. there was little or no variability in earnings among sets of twins with the same level of education
   b. there was little or no variability in earnings among sets of twins with different levels of education
   c.* individual twins with more education exhibited higher earnings than their twin sibling with less education
   d. twins exhibited age-earnings profiles that are not consistent with the human capital model

35. (*World of Work* 4-2) Research by James *et. al.* indicates that starting salaries of college graduates are influenced most by:
   a. whether one attended a private or a public college
   b. whether one attended a large university or a small college
   c. the geographic location of the college attended
   d.* choice of major and academic performance

36. (*World of Work* 4-3) In the German system of apprenticeships:
   a.* firms bear most of the training costs and trainees tend to remain attached to these firms after training
   b. firms bear most of the training costs and trainees tend to leave these firms after training
   c. apprentices bear most of the training costs and then tend to remain attached to the firms that trained them
   d. apprentices bear most of the training costs and then tend to leave the firms that trained them

37. (*World of Work* 4-4) Marxists believe that the U. S. education system functions so as to:
   a. train future managers how to form labor unions
   b. create a highly skilled but unprofitable work force
   c. teach "good" students to think and act independently
   d.* generate a disciplined, obedient, and well-motivated workforce

CHAPTER 5
The Demand for Labor

       C.   Personal Computers
       D.   Minimum Wage
       E.   Bank Tellers
       F.   Defense Cutbacks

WORLD OF WORK
       1.   Comparative Advantage and the Demand for Labor
       2.   The Rising Demand for Contingent Workers

GLOBAL PERSPECTIVES
       1.   Annual Net Employment Change as a Percentage of Total Employment, 1984 – 94
       2.   Part-time Employment as a Percentage of Total Employment, 1995
       3.   Temporary Employment as a Percentage of Total Employment

APPENDIX: ISOQUANT-ISOCOST ANALYSIS OF THE LONG-RUN DEMAND FOR LABOR
       A.   Isoquant Curves
            1.   Downward Slope
            2.   Convexity to the Origin
            3.   Higher Output to the Northeast
       B.   Isocost Curves
       C.   Least-Cost Combination of Capital and Labor
       D.   Deriving the Long-run Labor Demand Curve

LEARNING OBJECTIVES

After learning the material in Chapter 5 of *Contemporary Labor Economics*, the student should be able to:

1. define and use correctly the terms "derived demand", "marginal product", "average product", "total product", "zone of production", and "elasticity of labor demand"

2. graph and explain the relationships between the total, marginal, and average product curves

3. explain the law of diminishing marginal productivity and how it affects labor demand curves

4. derive the marginal revenue product schedule from the product demand and marginal product of labor schedules

5. explain why the marginal revenue product of labor is the basis for labor demand in the short run

6. distinguish between competitive and monopolistic output markets, and how the difference influences labor demand

7. explain the difference between short-run and long-run labor demand

8. using the concepts "output effect" and "substitution effect," explain why a firm's long-run demand for labor is more elastic than its short-run demand

9. distinguish between "substitutes in production" and "gross substitutes"

10. distinguish between "complements in production" and "gross complements"

11. derive the market demand curve for labor, and explain why it is generally more inelastic than the simple summation of the labor demand curves of all firms in the market

12. identify the determinants of the elasticity of labor demand

13. identify the determinants of the demand for labor

14. (appendix) use isoquant/isocost analysis to determine the combination of inputs that minimizes total costs for a given level of output produced

15. (appendix) graphically derive a firm's labor demand curve using isoquant/isocost analysis

ANSWERS TO SELECTED END-OF-CHAPTER QUESTIONS

2. In competitive markets, AP > MP implies that labor costs exceed total revenue; the firm should shut down in the short run.

4.

Wage	Quantity	VMP
$18	0	
14	1	$17.00
11	2	13.50
6	3	10.40
2	4	7.00
1	5	4.55

5. a. Demand will shift to the right.
    b. Demand will shift to the right.
    c. Demand will shift to the left.

10. Total wage bill: at a $6 wage, the bill is $18; at an $11 wage, the bill is $22
    Demand is inelastic, $E_d = .68$.

(Appendix)
5. Quantity of capital increased; the substitution effect (of capital for labor) exceeds the output effect.

6. Unit elastic.

MULTIPLE CHOICE QUESTIONS

Questions 1-6 are based on the short-run production function below.

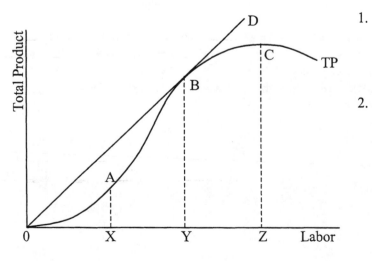

1. The "zone of production" consists of labor inputs over the range of:
   a. 0X   c. 0Y
   b.* YZ   d. XZ

2. The slope of line segment OD can be interpreted as the:
   a. total product of labor at Y
   b.* average product of labor at Y
   c. marginal product of labor over the range 0Y
   d. greatest possible marginal product of labor

3. The slope of line segment 0D can be interpreted as the:
   - a.* marginal product of labor at Y
   - b. total product of labor over the range 0Y
   - c. marginal product of labor over the range 0Y
   - d. the greatest possible total product of labor

4. Between X and Y:
   - a.* the marginal product of labor is falling, but is greater than average product
   - b. both the marginal product and the average product of labor are falling
   - c. marginal product is rising and average product is falling
   - d. both the marginal product and the average product of labor are rising

5. The "law of diminishing marginal returns" begins to take effect at labor input level:
   - a. 0
   - b.* X
   - c. Y
   - d. Z

6. At point C:
   - a. average product is maximized
   - c.* marginal product is zero
   - b. marginal product is maximized
   - d. total product is zero

7. Which of the following equalities holds when the profit-maximizing quantity of labor is employed in the short-run?
   - a.* MRP = MWC
   - c. MRP = AP
   - b. MP = wage rate
   - d. MRP = 0

8. The short-run labor demand curve of a competitive firm is:
   - a. its average revenue product curve
   - b.* its marginal revenue product curve, provided marginal product is below average product
   - c. its marginal product curve
   - d. stage II of the total product curve

9. Which of the following best describes the "law of diminishing marginal returns"?
   - a. the marginal product of labor is negative
   - b. output per worker must eventually fall
   - c. as more labor is added to a fixed stock of capital, total output must eventually fall
   - d.* as more labor is added to a fixed stock of capital, labor's marginal product must eventually fall

10. Value of marginal product (VMP) differs from marginal revenue product (MRP) in that:
    - a. MRP measures the value society places on the next worker's output while VMP measures the value the firm places on the next worker's output
    - b.* VMP measures the value society places on the next worker's output while MRP measures the value the firm places on the next worker's output
    - c. MRP always exceeds VMP
    - d. VMP always exceeds MRP

Questions 11 – 18 are based on the data in the following table. Assume that the labor market is perfectly competitive.

Labor	Output	Price (D_1)	Price (D_2)
0	0	$10.00	$10.00
1	15	10.00	9.50
2	29	10.00	9.00
3	42	10.00	8.50
4	54	10.00	7.50
5	65	10.00	6.50
6	75	10.00	5.50

11. Suppose product demand is given by the column labeled D_1. If the wage rate is $100, the firm will achieve maximum profit by hiring _____ workers.
    a. 3   c. 5
    b. 4   d.* 6

12. Suppose product demand is given by the column labeled D_1. If the wage rate rises from $100 to $130, the firm will reduce the quantity of labor employed by _____ unit(s)
    a. 0   b. 1   c.* 2   d. 3

13. Suppose product demand is given by the column labeled D_1. If the wage rate is $120, the firm will achieve maximum profit by hiring _____ workers.
    a. 3   b.* 4   c. 5   d. 6

14. Suppose product demand is given by the column labeled D_1. The value of the marginal product of the fourth worker is:
    a. $10   b. $54   c.* $120   d. $540

15. Suppose product demand is given by the column labeled D_2. If the wage rate is $100, the firm will achieve maximum profit by hiring _____ workers
    a.* 2   b. 3   c. 4   d. 5

16. Suppose product demand is given by the column labeled D_2. The extra revenue generated by the fourth worker is:
    a. $1   b. $12   c.* $48   d. $405

17. Suppose product demand is given by the column labeled D_2. If the wage rate rises from $100 to $130, the firm will reduce the quantity of labor employed by _____ unit(s).
    a. 0   b.* 1   c. 2   d. 3

18. Compared to D_1, a firm facing demand schedule D_2 will hire:
    a.   the same number of workers, since total product is the same in both instances
    b.*   fewer workers, since product price declines as output increases
    c.   more workers, since product price declines as output increases
    d.   more information is required

19. The marginal revenue product schedule:
    a.   measures the increase in total revenue that results from the production of one more unit
    b.   measures the decline in product price that a firm must accept in order to sell the extra output of one more worker
    c.   is the same whether the firm is selling in a purely competitive or imperfectly competitive market
    d.*   is the firm's labor demand schedule, provided the firm is operating in the zone of production

Questions 20 – 23 are based on the data in the following table. Assume that the labor market is perfectly competitive.

Labor	Output	Price
0	0	$2.20
1	15	2.00
2	29	1.80
3	42	1.60
4	54	1.40
5	65	1.20

20.   If the wage is $20.00, how many workers will this profit-maximizing firm choose to employ?
a.*   2   c.   4
b.   3.   d.   5

21.   What are the value of marginal product and the marginal revenue product, respectively, for the fourth worker?
a. $67.20; $9.60   c.* $12.60; $4.80
b. $12.60; $9;60   d. $67.20; $62.40

22.   If the wage is $11.00, how many workers will this profit-maximizing firm choose to employ?
a.   2   b.*   3   c.   4   d.   5

23.   Rather than the product demand schedule shown in the table, suppose this firm sold its output competitively for a price of $2.00. In this case, how many workers will this profit-maximizing firm choose to employ at a wage of $11.00?
a.   2   b.   3.   c.   4   d.*   5

24.   "The extra output, measured in dollars, that accrues to society when an additional unit of labor is employed" best describes:
a.   marginal product   c.*   value of marginal product
b.   marginal revenue product   d.   total revenue product

25.   For a firm selling output in an imperfectly competitive market, its labor demand curve will:
a.   reflect the value of marginal product schedule, provided the firm is operating in the zone of production
b.   decline solely because of diminishing marginal productivity
c.*   decline because of diminishing marginal productivity and because product price declines as output increases
d.   be perfectly elastic if the firm is hiring labor competitively

26.   "To find the market demand curve for a particular type of labor, simply sum the labor demand curves of all employers of that type of labor." This statement is:
a.   true
b.   false—sum the value of marginal product curves for the firms to account for changes in wage rates as employment increases
c.   false—sum the value of marginal product curves for the firms to account for changes in output price as production increases
d.*   false—although the price of output for any individual firm may be constant, this may not be the case for all firms taken collectively

27. Which of the following best describes the output effect of a wage increase?
    a.* The firm's marginal cost increases, the firm desires to produce less output, and therefore less labor is required
    b. The cost of labor is relatively higher causing the firm to use relatively more capital and less labor
    c. The firm's marginal cost falls, the firm desires to produce more output, and therefore more labor is required
    d. The firm's labor demand curve becomes more inelastic, causing it to employ less labor

28. Which of the following best describes the substitution effect of a wage increase?
    a. The firm's marginal cost increases, the firm desires to produce less output, and therefore less labor is required
    b.* The cost of labor is relatively higher causing the firm to use relatively more capital and less labor
    c. The firm's labor demand curve less elastic, causing it to employ less labor
    d. The firm's labor demand curve becomes more inelastic, causing it to employ less labor

29. The short-run labor demand curve is typically:
    a.* less elastic than the long-run labor demand curve
    b. the same as the long-run labor demand curve
    c. more elastic than the long-run labor demand curve
    d. more elastic than the long-run labor demand curve only if labor and capital are gross complements

30. Suppose that, as a result of an decrease in the market supply of labor, the wage rate has risen 10%. After adjusting their employment levels, firms find their total wage bill has decreased. This occurrence indicates that labor demand:
    a. is inelastic over this range of wages
    b.* is elastic over this range of wages
    c. is unit elastic over this range of wages
    d. was inelastic at the old wage, but is elastic at the new, higher wage

31. Suppose that, as a result of an increase in the market supply of labor, the wage rate has fallen 10%. After adjusting their employment levels, firms find their total wage bill has decreased. This occurrence indicates that labor demand:
    a.* is inelastic over this range of wages
    b. is elastic over this range of wages
    c. is unit elastic over this range of wages
    d. was inelastic at the old wage, but is elastic at the new, higher wage

32. In comparing two otherwise identical industries X and Y, an economist finds that labor demand is more elastic in industry X. Which of the following would support this finding?
    a. Capital and labor are less easily substituted for one another in X than in Y
    b. Labor costs as a percentage of total costs are relatively lower in X than in Y
    c.* Product demand elasticity is higher in X than in Y
    d. Substitute resources have a less elastic supply in X than in Y

35

33. Assume that skilled labor and energy are substitutes in production. An increase in energy prices is then predicted to:
   a. unambiguously increase the demand for skilled labor
   b. unambiguously decrease the demand for skilled labor
   c increase the demand for skilled labor if the output effect outweighs the substitution effect
   d.* decrease the demand for skilled labor if the output effect outweighs the substitution effect

34. If energy and unskilled labor are gross complements, an increase in the price of energy will:
   a. increase the supply of unskilled labor, decreasing the unskilled wage
   b. increase the demand for unskilled labor, raising the unskilled wage
   c.* decrease the demand for unskilled labor, decreasing the unskilled wage
   d. either increase or decrease the demand for unskilled labor, depending on the relative strengths of the output effect and the substitution effect

35. Skilled labor will benefit from an increase in the wage rate paid to unskilled labor if:
   a.* the substitution effect outweighs the output effect
   b. the output effect outweighs the substitution effect
   c. the output effect and substitution effect work in opposite directions
   d. skilled labor and unskilled labor are gross complements

36. (*World of Work* 5-1) International trade:
   a.* increases labor demand in some industries, reduces it in others
   b. reduces the overall demand for labor
   c. increases the overall demand for labor
   d. has no impact on labor demand at all

37. (*World of Work* 5-2) The contingent work force:
   a. makes up about one-tenth of the U.S. labor force
   b. includes only temporary workers
   c.* includes both voluntary and involuntary part-time workers
   d. has shrunk relative to the "core" labor force

38. (*World of Work* 5-3) Research by Farber indicates that consequences of job loss, such as continued unemployment and earnings losses:
   a. worsened in the 1980s, particularly among women
   b.* are substantial, but have not increased over time
   c. have equal impacts on workers at all education levels
   d. are of little consequence, since most workers eventually find equivalent jobs

39. (appendix) An isoquant shows all combinations of:
   a. wage rates and per unit costs of capital that yield the same total profit
   b. labor and capital that yield the same total profit
   c. labor and capital that yield the same total cost
   d.* labor and capital that yield the same total output

40. (appendix) At the least-cost combination of capital and labor:
   a.* the marginal rate of technical substitution of labor for capital equals the ratio of the price of labor to the price of capital
   b. the isocost line cuts the isoquant at its lowest point
   c. the capital-labor ratio is equal to the ratio of the price of labor to the price of capital
   d. is isoquant cuts the isocost line at its lowest point

41. (appendix) The slope of an isoquant reflects the:
    a. elasticity of demand for labor
    b. isocost line
    c. price of capital relative to labor
    d.* marginal rate of technical substitution

42. (appendix) If the marginal rate of technical substitution of labor for capital is greater than the price of labor relative to capital, then the firm can produce the same level of output at lower total cost by using:
    a. more capital and less labor   c. more capital and more labor
    b.* less capital and more labor   d. less capital and less labor

Questions 43 and 44 refer to the following graph:

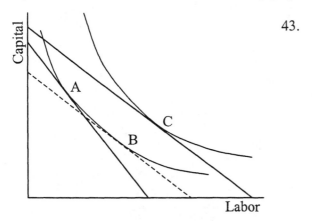

43. (appendix) If the two isoquants represent profit maximizing levels of output for two different wage rates, the move from point A to point B represents the:
    a. output effect of a reduction in the wage
    b. output effect of an increase in the wage
    c.* substitution effect of a reduction in the wage
    d. substitution effect of an increase in the wage

44. (appendix) If the two isoquants represent profit maximizing levels of output for two different wage rates, the output effect of a decrease in the wage rate is represented by the move from:
    a. A to B   c. A to C
    b.* B to C   d. C to A

CHAPTER 6
Wage Determination and the Allocation of Resources

LEARNING OBJECTIVES

After learning the material in Chapter 6 of *Contemporary Labor Economics*, the student should be able to:

1. define and use correctly the terms "marginal wage cost" and "allocative efficiency"

2. list the characteristics of a perfectly competitive labor market

3. explain why a market labor supply curve slopes upward and to the right, although individual labor supply curves are normally backward bending

4. list the determinants of labor supply and demand; for a change in any one, predict the impact on the equilibrium wage rate and employment level

5. determine and show graphically the profit-maximizing level of employment for a firm hiring labor form a perfectly competitive labor market

6. describe the conditions necessary for allocative efficiency and explain why competitive product and labor markets achieve those conditions

7. use production and demand data to derive and plot a monopolist's short-run demand for labor curve and explain why labor demand is more inelastic in this case than when the firm sells its output in a perfectly competitive market

8. explain why a firm with monopoly power hires less labor than if it sold its output in a competitive market

9. graphically determine a monopsonist's wage and employment level and show the efficiency loss associated with that employment level

10. explain why a firm with monopsony power hires less labor than a firm hiring labor in a competitive market

11. describe why a monopsonist may perceive a labor shortage where in fact there is none

12. summarize the several techniques that unions use to raise the wages of their members

13. explain wage and employment outcomes of unionized labor markets

14. explain why the wage and employment outcomes are indeterminate in a bilateral monopoly market structure

15. explain why labor markets characterized by delayed supply responses may exhibit a cobweb-shaped adjustment path to equilibrium

ANSWERS TO SELECTED END-OF-CHAPTER QUESTIONS

3. Labor demand will increase in cases (a), (c), and (d); labor demand will decrease in cases (b), (e), and (g); the quantity of labor demanded will increase in case (f).

4. a. The wage rate may either rise or fall, but employment will rise.
    b. Both the wage rate and employment fall.

6. b. 4 in X; 5 in Y; $131.
    c. No: the value of labor's marginal product in Y exceeds that in X. The efficient allocation of labor is 2 units in X and 3 units in Y.
    d. $P_L > VMP$ in each use; 0 in each use; $98 (=25 x 9 - 127).
    e. $12; 12.

7.	L	TWC	MWC		a.	The labor market is competitive, but the product market is characterized by some monopoly power.
	1	$10	$10		b.	4 workers.
	2	20	10		c.	No: VMP exceeds MWC.
	3	30	10			
	4	40	10			
	5	50	10			
	6	60	10			

8. a.   4.
    b. $4.
    c.   monopsony.

10.   Inelastic demand.

13.   Each makes labor demand more inelastic.

MULTIPLE CHOICE QUESTIONS

1. Which one of the following is generally considered a characteristic of a perfectly competitive labor market?
    a.   A few workers of varying skills and capabilities
    b.   Wage-setting behavior by firms
    c.* Numerous firms hiring labor from the same pool of qualified workers
    d.   Costly information

2. Which of the following best explains why the *market* labor supply curve is upward sloping, even though *individual* supply curves are normally backward bending?
    a.   The statement is not true: market labor supply curves are also backward bending
    b.   Market labor supply curves are "price-adjusted," whereas individual supply curves are not
    c.   Lower wages in a given market increase the demand for labor, so more labor must be supplied to maintain labor market equilibrium
    d.* Higher wages in a given market attract more workers away from other activities, more than compensating for any reduction in hours by individuals already in the market

3. In a perfectly competitive environment, the height of the market labor supply curve at any given number of labor hours indicates:
    a.   the total cost of employing that number of hours in the given occupation
    b.   the marginal cost of employing the first hour of labor
    c.* the value of the alternative activity in which the marginal hour might otherwise be used
    d.   the maximum wage employers would be willing to pay to attract the marginal hour from its alternate use

4. The profit maximizing employer will obtain its optimal level of employment where:
    a.   marginal revenue product equals value of marginal product
    b.* marginal revenue product equals marginal wage cost
    c.   value of marginal product equals marginal wage cost
    d.   marginal product equals marginal revenue product

41

Questions 5 – 9 refer to the following diagram of a perfectly competitive labor market:

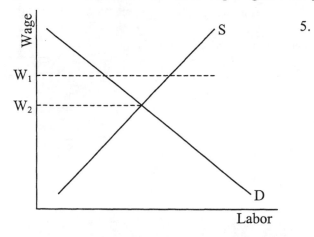

5.   At wage rate W_1 there is an:
a.*   excess supply of labor and the wage rate will fall
b.   excess supply of labor and the wage rate will rise
c.   excess demand for labor and the wage rate will fall
d.   excess demand for labor and the wage rate will rise

6.   For the supply and demand curves in the diagram, the level of employment will be highest at:
a.   wage rate W_1 c.   a wage rate higher than W_1
b.*   wage rate W_2 d.   a wage rate lower than W_2

7.   If the wage rate is W_2 and capital and labor are gross complements, then an increase in the cost of capital will:
a.   increase the supply of labor and drive the wage down
b.*   decrease the demand for labor and drive the wage down
c.   increase the demand for labor and drive the wage up
d.   either increase or decrease the demand for labor depending on whether the substitution effect or the output effect is stronger

8.   Suppose workers in this labor market (X) are qualified to work in an alternative competitive labor market (Y), and vice versa. An increase in the demand for labor in market Y will:
a.   increase labor supply in X and drive its wage down
b.*   decrease labor supply in X and drive its wage up
c.   reduce labor supply in Y and drive its wage down
d.   have no impact at all in X

9.   A net increase in people's preferences for work versus leisure in this market will:
a.*   increase labor supply, reducing the wage rate
b.   decrease labor supply, increasing the wage rate
c.   increase labor demand, increasing the wage rate
d.   decrease labor demand, reducing the wage rate

10.   At the profit maximizing level of employment for a monopolist:
a.   marginal revenue product equals the value of marginal product
b.   marginal revenue product exceeds the value of marginal product
c.   value of marginal product equals the marginal wage cost
d.*   marginal revenue product is less than the value of marginal product

11.   All profit-maximizing firms hire labor up to the point where:
a.   price times marginal product equals the wage rate
b.   marginal revenue times marginal product equals the wage rate
c.   price times marginal product equals the marginal wage cost
d.*   marginal revenue times marginal product equals the marginal wage cost

Questions 12 and 13 refer to the following diagram:

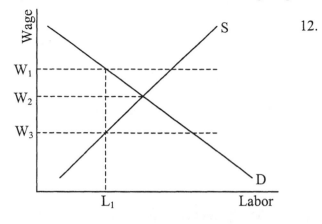

12. Suppose the wage is currently W_1 and L_1 is the level of employment. Then, the value of the last worker's additional output is _____ and the opportunity cost of the last worker's time is _____:

   a. $W_1; W_1$ c.* $W_1; W_3$
   b. $W_1; W_2$ d. $W_2; W_2$

13. Suppose the wage is currently W_3 and L_1 is the level of employment. Then we should expect the wage to:
   a.*   rise and employment to rise   c.   fall and employment to rise
   b.   rise and employment to fall   d.   fall and employment to fall

14. Which one of the following conditions is required for allocative efficiency?
   a.   Marginal revenue product exceeds the value of marginal product by the greatest amount
   b.   Marginal revenue product equals the wage rate
   c.   Value of marginal product equals the marginal wage cost
   d.*   Value of marginal product is the same in all alternative employments of labor

15. Allocative efficiency is achieved when:
   a.   the marginal product of labor equals its value of marginal product
   b.   all resources are fully employed
   c.   the price of each resource equals the value of its marginal product
   d.*   the price of each resource equals the value of its marginal product and its marginal opportunity cost

Questions 16 – 18 refer to the following table, that shows the short-run production relationship and the output demand relationship for a firm.

Labor	Output	Output Price
1	10	$20.00
2	15	19.00
3	19	18.00
4	22	17.00
5	24	16.00
6	25	15.00

16. The table indicates that:
   a.   the firm sells output in a perfectly competitive market
   b.*   the firm is a monopolist
   c.   the firm hires labor in a perfectly competitive market
   d.   the firm is a monopsonist

17. How many workers will this firm hire if the wage is $10?
   a.   3   b.   4   c.*   5   d.   6

18. What is the value of the third worker's marginal product?
   a. $18   b. $57   c.* $72   d. $342

19. For firms in competitive labor markets:
    a.* $P_L = MWC$ and $VMP = MRP$ c. $P_L > MWC$ and $VMP = MRP$
    b. $P_L = MWC$ and $VMP > MRP$ d. $P_L > MWC$ and $VMP > MRP$

20. Which of the following is a *true* statement?
    a.   Monopolists employ too many labor resources, because the value of the marginal product exceeds the marginal opportunity cost of labor
    b.   For a monopolist, the marginal revenue product of labor exceeds marginal wage at the profit maximizing level of employment
    c.   Monopolists pay a lower wage than competitors for the same type of labor
    d.* The monopolist's demand for labor curve is less elastic than if it were a competitor in the sale of its output.

Questions 21 – 23 refer to the following diagram that shows the labor demand for a monopolistic firm hiring labor from a competitive labor market.

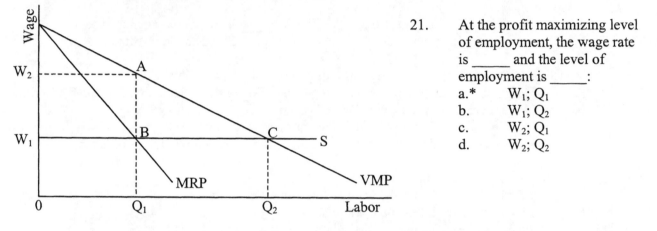

21. At the profit maximizing level of employment, the wage rate is _____ and the level of employment is _____:
    a.* $W_1; Q_1$
    b. $W_1; Q_2$
    c. $W_2; Q_1$
    d. $W_2; Q_2$

22. The efficiency loss associated with the profit maximizing wage and employment level is given by area:
    a. Q_1ACQ_2 b.*   BAC   c. $0W_2AQ_1$ d. W_1W_2AC

23. If anti-trust legislation forced the monopolist to behave like a "price-taker," then the firm would pay the wage rate _____ and the quantity of labor employed would be _____.
    a. $W_1; Q_1$ b.* $W_1; Q_2$ c. $W_2; Q_1$ d. $W_2; Q_2$

24. Compared to a firm that sells its output competitively, an otherwise identical monopolist will:
    a.   pay a lower wage   c.   pay a higher wage
    b.* pay the same wage   d.   may pay either a higher or lower wage

25. At the profit maximizing level of employment for a monopsonist:
    a.   the wage exceeds the marginal wage cost
    b.   marginal revenue product equals the wage
    c.* the wage is less than marginal wage cost
    d.   marginal product equals marginal revenue product

26. Compared to a monopsonist that sells its output in a competitive product market, an otherwise identical monopsonist with monopoly power in the product market will pay:
    a.* a lower wage   c.   the same wage
    b.   a higher wage   d.   more information is needed

27. A monopsonist's marginal wage cost curve is positively sloped because:
   a.   it "discriminates" by paying each worker a different wage according to his or her opportunity cost
   b.   it must charge a lower price for each additional unit of output, and it must charge this lower price for all units sold
   c.   it pays its workers lower wages, so that the supply of labor to the market is restricted
   d.*   it must pay a higher wage to attract additional workers, and it must pay this higher wage to all workers

Questions 28 – 30 refer to the following diagram of a monopsonistic labor market.

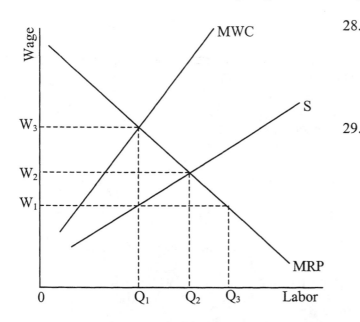

28. At the profit maximizing level of employment, the wage rate is _____ and the level of employment is _____:
   a.* $W_1; Q_1$ c. $W_2; Q_2$
   b. $W_3; Q_1$ d. $W_3; Q_3$

29. Relative to their monopsony levels, both the wage and the level of employment would increase in this market if a wage-setting union negotiates a wage:
   a.*   anywhere between W_1 and W_3
   b.   anywhere between W_2 and W_3
   c.   anywhere between W_1 and W_2
   d.   equal to W_2 only

30. If legislation set the minimum wage at W_2, then employment:
   a.   would fall from its original monopsony level
   b.   would remain unchanged
   c.*   would rise from its original monopsony level
   d.   may or may not change from its original monopsony level

31. Compared to the allocatively efficient amount, a monopsonist tends to hire:
   a.   too few workers because the value of marginal product exceeds marginal revenue product
   b.*   too few workers because marginal wage cost exceeds the wage rate
   c.   too many workers because the value of marginal product exceeds marginal revenue product
   d.   too many workers because marginal wage cost exceeds the wage rate

32. A union will most likely attempt to restrict the growth of labor supply if:
   a.   the labor supply curve is very inelastic
   b.*   the labor demand curve is very inelastic
   c.   there is a very slow rate of growth of labor demand
   d.   there is a very elastic supply of a production substitute for union labor

33. Which one of the following enhances a union's ability to bargain for an above-equilibrium wage rate for its members by restricting the growth of labor supply?
   a.   increased international competition from lower wage workers
   b.   offsetting increases in worker productivity
   c.   bilateral monopoly
   d.*   work rules that inhibit the ability of employers to assign workers to tasks

34. Which of the following actions might a union use to try to restrict the growth of labor supply?
   a.   Increase product demand
   b.*   Reduce the number of qualified workers
   c.   Enhance worker productivity
   d.   Reduce the wage for nonunion labor

35. A union might attempt to raise both the wage rate and employment of its members by:
   a.   lobbying for state licensing requirements for union jobs
   b.   arguing for easing of immigration restrictions
   c.*   launching an advertising campaign to encourage purchases of union-produced goods
   d.   attempting to raise the price of complementary inputs

36. In the absence of coalescing power, we expect that in bilateral monopoly:
   a.*   the resulting wage rate will depend on the relative bargaining strengths of the firm and the union
   b.   there will likely be greater efficiency loss than if there were market power on only one side of the market
   c.   the resulting employment level will be lower than if there were market power on only one side of the market
   d.   the resulting wage rate will be above the union's desired wage but below the monopsonist's desired wage

37. One criticism of the cobweb model is that:
   a.*   students form rational expectations of the effect of changes in labor demand and adjust their supply responses accordingly
   b.   the prediction of chronic boom-bust cycles is not borne out in the real world
   c.   students adjust career decisions based on starting salaries rather lifetime earnings
   d.   demand is likely to shift as the market approaches equilibrium, so that equilibrium is never achieved

Question 38 refers to the following diagram:

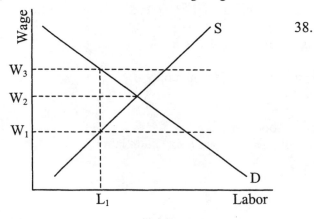

38. Suppose the wage is currently W_1 and L_1 is the level of employment. If this market is characterized by delayed supply responses, in the immediate period the wage will:
   a.   rise and employment will rise
   b.*   rise and employment will remain unchanged
   c.   remain unchanged and employment will rise
   d.   remain unchanged and employment will remain unchanged

46

39.   (*World of Work* 6-1) Which of the following is *not* a factor that helps to explain the stagnation of real wages over the 1979 – 1995 period?
        a.   Increased labor force participation of married women
        b.   Deregulation in key industries, such as airlines and trucking
        c.*   A sharp increase in unionization
        d.   Increased competition from foreigners in output markets

40.   (*World of Work* 6-2) Which of the following supports the view that U. S. chief executive officers (CEOs) are not overpaid?
        a.*   Good management enhances productivity throughout an entire organization
        b.   The ratio of CEO pay to average pay is no higher in the U. S. than in other industrial countries
        c.   There is little relationship between marginal revenue and pay for most workers, including CEOs
        d.   CEO pay is set by corporate boards, which act in the best interest of shareholders

41.   (*World of Work* 6-3) With respect to Major League Baseball, studies by Scully and Summers and Quinton found that:
        a.*   players were paid substantially less than their marginal revenue products prior to free agency
        b.   players were paid their marginal revenue products even before free agency, which is consistent with the competitive nature of the baseball business
        c.   players were paid their marginal revenue products prior to free agency. Since that time, salaries have fallen below marginal revenue products
        d.   salaries far exceed marginal revenue products since the advent of free agency

42.   (*World of Work* 6-4) Attempts by unionized city government workers to shift their labor demand curve have resulted in:
        a.   increased total city expenditures
        b.   increased demand for nonunionized employees in the same city
        c.*   increased employment of unionized workers
        d.   substantial reductions in union employment

43.   (*World of Work* 6-5) Which one of the following is a true statement?
        a.   Although theory suggests the decline of unionization should have increased income inequality, empirical research suggests that the opposite occurred
        b.   Although theory suggests the decline in unionization should have reduced income inequality, empirical research suggests that the opposite occurred
        c.*   In theory, the decline in unionization may either reduce or increase income inequality, however empirical research suggests it has increased it
        d.   In theory, the decline in unionization may either reduce or increase income inequality, however empirical research suggests it has reduced it

44.   (*World of Work* 6-6) In response to the argument that manufacturing jobs will be transferred from the U.S. to Mexico, advocates of NAFTA argue that:
        a.   the U.S. has an absolute advantage over Mexico in manufacturing, so no jobs will be lost
        b.   labor productivity is higher in Mexico than in the U.S., so the U.S. could not compete with Mexican manufacturing firms
        c.   lower tariffs will increase the demand for labor across the entire U.S. economy
        d.*   lower tariffs will enhance the competitiveness of exporting firms in the U.S., opening new markets to them, thereby increasing their demand for labor

CHAPTER 7
Alternative Pay Schemes and Labor Efficiency

I.   ECONOMICS OF FRINGE BENEFITS
    A.   Fringe Benefits: Facts
          1.   Fringe Benefits as a Proportion of Total Compensation
          2.   Fringe Benefit Growth

II. THEORY OF OPTIMAL FRINGE BENEFITS
    A.   Worker's Indifference Map
    B.   Employer's Isoprofit Curve
    C.   Wage-Fringe Optimum
    D.   Causes of Fringe Benefit Growth
          1.   Tax Advantages to the Employer
          2.   Economies of Scale
          3.   Efficiency Considerations
          4.   Other Factors

III. THE PRINCIPAL-AGENT PROBLEM

IV. PAY FOR PERFORMANCE
    A.   Piece Rates
    B.   Commissions and Royalties
    C.   Raises and Promotions
          1.   Salaries and Work Incentives
               a.   Hourly Pay
               b.   Annual Salary
          2.   Solution: Raises and Promotions
    D.   Bonuses
          1.   Personal Performance
          2.   Team Performance
    E.   Profit Sharing
    F.   Tournament Pay

V.   EFFICIENCY WAGE PAYMENTS
    A.   Wage-Productivity Dependency
          1.   Shirking Model of Efficiency Wages
          2.   Other Efficiency Wage Theories
               a.   Nutritional Model
               b.   Labor Turnover Model
    B.   Implication: Nonclearing Labor Markets
    C.   Criticisms

VI. DEFERRED PAYMENT SCHEMES
    A.   Seniority Pay
    B.   Role of Pensions
    C.   Deferred Contracts: Some Final Points

VII.   LABOR MARKET EFFICIENCY REVISITED

WORLD OF WORK
     1.   Does Health Insurance Cause "Job Lock"?
     2.   The Fall in Private-Sector Pension Coverage Among Men
     3.   Principals and Agents: "Solutions" as Problems
     4.   Why is there Academic Tenure?
     5.   The Fort Motor Company's $5 Per Day Wage

GLOBAL PERSPECTIVE
     1.   Pension Coverage, 1987 – 1989
     2.   Percentage of Workers in a Profit-Sharing Plan, 1992 – 1993

LEARNING OBJECTIVES

After learning the material in Chapter 7 of *Contemporary Labor Economics*, the student should be able to:

1.   describe the growth and variation in fringe benefits by industry and occupation

2.   explain how the wage-fringe trade-off can be represented by indifference and isoprofit curves; graphically depict the wage-fringe optimum

3.   show, with reference to indifference and isoprofit curves, why there has been growth in fringe benefits

4.   describe the principal-agent problem as it applies to the employer-employee relationship

5.   explain the advantages and disadvantages associated with piece rate wages, commissions and royalties, and time rate wages

6.   use graphical analysis to explain why salaried workers have an incentive to shirk and how the compensation plan can be structured to minimize this activity

7.   explain, with reference to the principal-agent and free-rider problems, some of the difficulties of implementing an effective bonus or profit-sharing plan.

8.   explain how high pay for senior executives may improve efficiency

9.   explain why a firm may choose to pay its workers more than the market-clearing wage

10.   describe the shirking, nutritional, and labor-turnover models of efficiency wages

11.   explain why the payment of efficiency wages may result in nonclearing labor markets

12.   describe the roles of seniority and pensions in deferred payment schemes

13.   explain why implicit contracts tend to be self-enforcing

14.   correlate the existence of deferred payment schemes with firm size and monitoring costs

15.   refine the definition of efficiency to include compensation issues

ANSWERS TO SELECTED END-OF-CHAPTER QUESTIONS

3.   Indifference curves would likely be flatter with no change in the slope of the isoprofit curve. The likely effect would be to reduce the proportion of total compensation paid as fringe benefits.

5.   a.   Income variability; difficulty of attributing output to a single individual; other goals (quality, for example, or team cooperation) may suffer.
            b.   Free-riding.

12.   Nonwage income would rise, leading to a pure income effect on labor supply.

MULTIPLE CHOICE QUESTIONS

1.   "Total compensation" includes:
     a.*   Wages and salaries and all fringe benefits
     b.   Wages and salaries and public (legally mandated) fringe benefits only
     c.   Wages and salaries and private (nonmandatory) fringe benefits only
     d.   Wages and salaries and all fringe benefits net of all personal taxes

2.   The proportion of total compensation paid out as fringe benefits tends to be larger in:
     a.*   high-paid industries compared to low-paid industries
     b.   service industries compared to manufacturing industries
     c.   white-collar occupations compared to blue-collar occupations
     d.   retail trade compared to transportation and public utilities

3.   Fringe benefits currently account for approximately what percentage of total compensation?
     a.   5% – 10%   c.*   25% – 30%
     b.   15% – 20%   d.   35% – 40%

4   The share of fringe benefits in employee compensation:
     a.   grew steadily in the 1960s and 1970s but has fallen since 1980
     b.   was unchanged in the 1960s and 1970s and has fallen since 1980
     c.   shrank in the 1960s and 1970s and grew in the 1980s
     d.*   grew steadily in the 1960s and 1970s and continued to grow in the 1980s and 1990s

5.   Which one of the following is *inconsistent* with the proposition that workers may prefer an extra dollar's worth of fringe benefits to an extra dollar's worth of cash?
     a.   workers may prefer to bind themselves against their own tendencies toward immediate gratification
     b.   certain fringe benefits effectively trade current taxes for future taxes
     c.*   people generally prefer in-kind benefits to cash
     d.   certain fringe benefits are untaxed

6.   The slope of the wage-fringe isoprofit curve reflects:
     a.   the overall profitability of the firm
     b.   a worker's willingness to give up an extra dollar of wages in exchange for an extra dollar of fringe benefits
     c.*   the firm's cost of paying an extra dollar of compensation as wages rather than fringe benefits
     d.   an increasing marginal rate of substitution of fringe benefits for cash

7.　The slope of a wage-fringe indifference curve reflects:
　　a.　the overall utility level of a person
　　b.*　a worker's willingness to give up an extra dollar of wages in exchange for an extra dollar of fringe benefits
　　c.　the firm's cost of paying an extra dollar of compensation as wages rather than fringe benefits
　　d.　an increasing marginal rate of substitution of fringe benefits for cash

8.　The firm's wage-fringe isoprofit curve typically has a slope less than 1 (absolute value) because:
　　a.　fringe benefits confer tax advantages on workers
　　b.　on average, it costs firms more to purchase fringe benefits than workers
　　c.*　the composition of fringe benefits may increase worker productivity
　　d.　the composition of fringe benefits reduces a firm's profit level

9.　The employer's share of the Social Security and Medicare components of the payroll tax has increased, from 6.13% in 1980 to its current rate of 7.65%. Because employers pay no payroll tax on many fringe benefits, this change in tax rates has effectively:
　　a.　reduced the "price" of fringe benefits, rotating the wage-fringe isoprofit line inward
　　b.　increased the "price" of fringe benefits, rotating the wage-fringe isoprofit line inward
　　c.*　reduced the "price" of fringe benefits, rotating the wage-fringe isoprofit line outward
　　d.　increased the "price" of fringe benefits, rotating the wage-fringe isoprofit line outward

10.　The trend of fringe benefits as a percentage of total compensation can be partially explained by the fact that:
　　a.　tax reform has rendered many types of fringe benefits fully taxable
　　b.　"in-kind" benefits restrict workers' consumption choices
　　c.*　the firm may be able to purchase fringe benefits more cheaply than workers
　　d.　many types of fringe benefits are income inelastic

Questions 11 – 15 refer to the diagram below. All points along the ray 0P reflect a constant proportion of wages to fringe benefits.

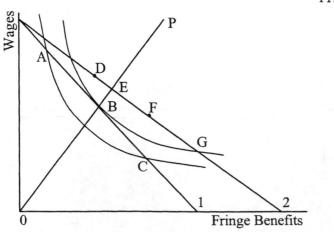

11.　The shape of the indifference curves reflects:
　　a.*　a diminishing marginal rate of substitution of fringe benefits for wages
　　b.　increased utility as fringe benefits are substituted for wages along an indifference curve
　　c.　increased utility as wages are substituted for fringe benefits along an indifference curve
　　d.　an increasing marginal rate of substitution of fringe benefits for wages

12.　Given isoprofit line 1, this worker's wage-fringe optimum is given by point:
　　a.　A　　　　b.*　B　　　　c.　C　　　　d.　D

13. Suppose some development rotates the isoprofit line outward, to line 2. If history is a guide, we would expect this worker's new wage-fringe optimum to be at point:
    a.   D   b.   E   c.*   F.   d.   G

14. Which one of the following events could *not* have caused a move from point B to point F?
    a.   The employer's share of the payroll tax rate has increased and the limits expanded
    b.   Firms structured fringe benefits so as to increase worker productivity
    c.*   The government changed tax laws such that some fringe benefits became taxable income to the worker
    d.   Insurance companies offered group discounts for medical and disability coverage

15. If the isoprofit line shifts from line 1 to line 2, then:
    a.   to maintain profit level 2 the firm must provide more fringe benefits and reduce wages
    b.   to maintain profit level 2 the firm must reduce fringe benefits and raise wages
    c.*   as the firm moves from line 1 to line 2 it could provide more fringe benefits while paying the same wage rate
    d.   providing more fringe benefits would reduce the firm's profit

16. Which of the following is *not* a cause of fringe benefit growth?
    a.   Tax advantages to the employer
    b.   Efficiency considerations
    c.   Economies of scale
    d.*   Fringe benefits are income inelastic

17. One view of the firm is that stockholders hire managers who, in turn, hire workers. Maximum profits are earned by satisfying the customer. The two principal/agent relationships illustrated in this view are:
    a.   manager-stockholder; worker-manager
    b.   stockholder-manager; customer-manager
    c.   manager-stockholder; manager-worker
    d.*   stockholder-manager; manager-worker

18. The principal-agent problem arises primarily because:
    a.   principals and agents work in a team, leading to free-rider problems
    b.   principals and agents have common interests
    c.   principals pursue some of their own objectives that may conflict with the objectives of the agents
    d.*   agents pursue some of their own objectives that may conflict with the objectives of the principals

19. Which one of the following best represents the principal-agent problem in the employer-employee relationship?
    a.   An employee works during a paid lunch hour in order to leave work one hour early
    b.   An employer fails to provide safety goggles to a worker as required by occupational safety and health legislation
    c.*   a worker leaves work early without permission
    d.   A worker opts for early retirement in response to the firm's incentive plan

20. Compensation paid in proportion to units of output sold best describes:
    a.   piece rates   c.   time rates
    b.*   commissions   d.   bonuses

21. From the employer's standpoint, the chief advantage of royalties and commissions is that this policy:
    a. promotes teamwork and cooperation
    b. increases turnover
    c.* reduces shirking where work effort is costly to observe
    d. reduces income variability

22. There is some controversy about profit-sharing plans because:
    a. potential free-rider problems render such plans ineffective in all but the largest firms
    b. profit-sharing is a type of deferred payment scheme
    c.* the link between profit-sharing and worker productivity is not always clear-cut
    d. there is no means by which greater work effort can be translated into greater compensation for a worker

23. Salaried workers can be considered "quasi-fixed resources" in that:
    a.* production is largely independent of the firm's use of salaried workers
    b. federal work rules limit the ability of firms to fire salaried workers
    c. their work hours typically are fixed
    d. raises or promotions may be used to reduce shirking

24. Raises and promotions are used by employers as a device to:
    a.* reduce shirking by salaried workers
    b. transform labor from a quasi-fixed to a variable resource
    c. reduce turnover by hourly workers
    d. reduce free-riding by teams of workers

25. A simple income-leisure model might predict that salaried workers would work fewer hours than hourly workers. In fact the opposite seems to be true, in part because:
    a.* raises and promotions are "won" on the basis of productivity rankings
    b. firms typically offer raises and promotions solely on the basis of seniority
    c. of the principle-agent problem
    d. salaried work is an example of a deferred compensation scheme

26. Team bonuses:
    a. solve the free-rider problem associated with individual bonuses
    b. create a principal-agent problem by channeling effort toward team performance at the expense of individual performance
    c. typically comprise a large percentage of the total compensation of middle managers, but almost none of the total pay of top executives
    d.* work best when targeted at relatively small groups of employees

27. In some instances, profit sharing may not be a very effective tool for raising worker productivity because of the:
    a.* free-rider problem
    b. principal-agent problem
    c. retirement problem
    d. tax and accounting rules that cause economic profit to differ from accounting profit

28. The free-rider problem is most likely to arise in:
    a.   small groups
    b.   firms that tie bonuses to individual performance
    c.*   a profit-sharing plan
    d.   firms that use piece rates

29. Tournament pay:
    a.   reduces profits because of the excessive pay to chief executive officers implied by such plans
    b.*   may help to rationalize why some ineffective senior executives continue to be employed by a firm
    c.   explains why "hostile" corporate takeovers occur
    d.   explains why chief executive officers typically serve long periods at the top of their companies

30. Raises and promotions may be viewed as a form of:
    a.   profit-sharing   c.   piece rate pay
    b.   commissions and royalties   d.*   tournament pay

Questions 31 – 32 refer to the following information. Suppose a "fully effective" worker can produce 20 units per hour in a particular firm. The firm's wage-productivity relationship is:

Wage	Output per Worker
$10	20
9	20
8	16
7	10

31. If the actual wage is $7, the wage cost per effective unit of labor is:
    a. $3.50   c. $7.00
    b. $10.00   d.* $14.00

32. This firm's efficiency wage rate is:
    a. $7.00   b. $8.00   c.* $9.00   d. $10.00

33. A firm might choose to pay its employees a wage higher than that which would clear the market because:
    a.*   the higher wage raises the opportunity cost of shirking
    b.   the higher wage may shift the labor demand curve to the left
    c.   the firm will have higher turnover, allowing new workers to invigorate the work place
    d.   the higher wage solves the free-rider problem

34. One implication of efficiency wage models is that:
    a.   firms pay wages below the market-clearing rate
    b.*   an excess supply of labor may be created
    c.   an excess demand for labor may be created
    d.   CEO contracts will contain golden parachute clauses

35. Which one of the following is *not* typically offered as an explanation for efficiency wages?
    a.*   An employer will not pay a wage that exceeds the market rate
    b.   A higher wage may reduce turnover
    c.   A higher wage may allow lower income workers to afford better nutrition that increases their stamina
    d.   The higher wage may be perceived by workers as raising the opportunity cost of shirking

36. Implicit contracts tend to:
   a. apply only to unionized workers
   b. apply only to nonunionized workers
   c.* apply to workers who have received specific training
   d. apply to workers who have received general training

37. Deferred payment schemes benefit the firm by:
   a. increasing turnover
   b.* inhibiting shirking where monitoring costs are high
   c. providing the proper incentives for older workers to retire
   d. giving older workers incentives to keep on working

38. Deferred payment schemes are more likely to occur at larger, well-known firms because:
   a. it is more difficult for smaller firms to monitor workers
   b. monitoring costs do not vary with firm size
   c.* smaller firms are more likely to go bankrupt
   d. better known firms are more likely to cheat on pension commitments

39. Deferred payment schemes may create a "retirement problem" because:
   a. the large pensions usually available with these schemes encourage highly productive executives to retire too soon
   b. workers wish to retire too soon since the wages of older workers fall below their marginal revenue products
   c.* older workers are typically paid wages above their marginal revenue products, reducing their incentive to retire
   d. workers covered by these plans typically wish to retire at age 62, but full Social Security benefits are not available until age 65

40. To solve the retirement problem created by deferred payment schemes, firms typically:
   a. require workers to stay until age 70
   b. "backload" pensions and defer vesting
   c.* provide a relatively large pension benefit upon retirement
   d. cancel pensions

41. Labor market efficiency requires that each worker be allocated to:
   a. the job offering the highest wage available
   b. the job offering the best fringe benefits available
   c. his or her optimal job
   d.* his or her optimal job, and that each firm implements its optimal compensation package

42. (*World of Work* 7-1) In their study of "job lock," Buchmueller and Valetta conclude:
   a. there is no empirical relationship between health insurance coverage and job lock
   b. health insurance coverage reduces job mobility for men but not for women
   c. job lock is greatest among those who use health care the least
   d.* "continuation of coverage" mandates increase job mobility by approximately 10%

43. (*World of Work* 7-2) According to research by Even and Macpherson, the fall in private-sector pension coverage among men is:
   a.   concentrated among men with higher earnings, who have substituted individual retirement accounts for pensions
   b.   offset by contributions to 401(k) plans, particularly for low-wage men
   c.   of little concern, since it has largely been offset by large increases in real wages
   d.*   due in large part to declining unionization

44. (*World of Work* 7-3) Solutions to principal-agent problems often create new problems. Which of the following is *not* a problem created by a principal-agent "solution?"
   a.   Sales incentives may harm customers
   b.   Production quotas may alienate workers
   c.*   Sales incentives fail to increase sales
   d.   Production quotas lead workers to find new ways to increase joint product

45. (*World of Work* 7-4) According to Carmichael, academic tenure has persisted because:
   a.   faculty have gained this fringe benefit through collective bargaining
   b.   college and university administrators see tenure as a way of discouraging their most productive senior faculty from retiring early
   c.   college and university administrators see tenure as a way to keep their most productive junior faculty from being recruited by rival schools
   d.*   senior faculty can identify promising new faculty without fear of losing their jobs

46. (*World of Work* 7-5) In 1914 Ford Motor Company doubled the wage it paid its employees, resulting in:
   a.   unusually high quit rates and absenteeism
   b.   no change in the number of job applicants, because the offer only applied to persons employed at Ford more than six months
   c.   lower quit rates and less absenteeism but no change in worker productivity
   d.*   an increase in worker productivity of more than 50%

CHAPTER 8
The Wage Structure

I.   PERFECT COMPETITION: HOMOGENEOUS WORKERS AND JOBS

II.   THE WAGE STRUCTURE; OBSERVED DIFFERENTIALS

III. WAGE DIFFERENTIALS: HETEROGENEOUS JOBS
      A.   Compensating Differentials
            1.   Risk of Job Injury or Death
            2.   Fringe Benefits
            3.   Job Status
            4.   Job location
            5.   Job Security: Regularity of Earnings
            6.   Prospect of Wage Advancement
            7.   Extent of Control over the Work Pace
      B.   Differing Skill Requirements
      C.   Differences Based on Efficiency Wage Payments
            1.   Shirking Model and Wage Differentials
            2.   Turnover Model and Wage Differentials
            3.   Preliminary Empirical findings
      D.   Other Job or Employer Heterogenties
            1.   Union Status
            2.   Tendency to Discriminate
            3.   Absolute and Relative Firm Size

IV.   WAGE DIFFERENTIALS: HETEROGENEOUS WORKERS
      A.   Differing Human Capital: Noncompeting Groups
      B.   Differing Individual Preferences
            1.   Differences in Time Preferences
            2.   Tastes for Nonwage Aspects of Jobs

V.   THE HEDONIC THEORY OF WAGES
      A.   The Worker's Indifference Map
      B.   The Employer's Normal Profit Isoprofit Curve
      C.   Matching Workers with Jobs
      D.   Labor Market Implications

VI.   WAGE DIFFERENTIALS: LABOR MARKET IMPERFECTIONS
      A.   Imperfect Labor Market Information
            1.   Wage Rate Distributions
            2.   Lengthy Adjustment Periods
      B.   Immobilities
            1.   Geographic Immobilities
            2.   Institutional Immobilities
            3.   Sociological Immobilities

WORLD OF WORK
1. Wage Inequality and Skill-Biased Technological Change
2. Smoking is Bad for Your Financial Health
3. Wage Differentials: Married Versus Single Males
4. Compensating Pay for Shift Work
5. Placing a Value on Human Life

GLOBAL PERSPECTIVE
1. Hourly Pay around the World

LEARNING OBJECTIVES

After learning the material in Chapter 8 of *Contemporary Labor Economics*, the student should be able to:

1. identify sources of wage differentials arising from differences in job or employer characteristics and distinguish them from those that arise from worker differences

2. distinguish between "equilibrium" wage differentials and "transitional" wage differentials

3. describe how wage differentials may arise based on efficiency wage payments

4. use indifference curves to show a worker's preferences for wages and job safety; explain the shape of these indifference curves

5. use isoprofit curves to show a firm's ability to trade off job safety and wages to maintain a level of profitability; explain the shape of isoprofit curves

6. explain the roles of individual preferences and firm technology in establishing equilibrium wage differentials

7. show graphically the optimal wage rate-job safety combination, and explain its significance in the matching of workers to jobs

8. using the hedonic theory of wages, derive the expected observed relationship between wages and nonwage job attributes

9. explain why laws that mandate a minimum standard of job safety may reduce the utility of some workers

10. describe the role of labor immobilities and costly or imperfect information in observed wage differentials.

ANSWERS TO SELECTED END-OF-CHAPTER QUESTIONS

4. The increased status may provide additional utility, but will attract more labor to the affected occupation and reduce wage rates.

6. In the case of efficiency wages, employers push the wage rate above that which would clear the labor market. They do this, for example, to create an incentive for workers not to shirk. Both the cost to the firm of shirking behavior and the cost of monitoring workers vary across industries and occupations, so efficiency wages can result in persistent wage differentials across those industries and occupations.

10. This would be the case if nonwage amenities—job security, for example—in government jobs were more highly valued than their private sector counterparts.

MULTIPLE CHOICE QUESTIONS

1. Assuming workers and jobs are identical, if information is perfect and job search and migration are costless, then:
    a. labor may or may not flow among employers
    b.* labor will flow among employers until all wages are equal
    c. labor will flow among employers until all economic profits are zero, but wages may be unequal
    d. all firms will hire the same number of workers in equilibrium and pay them all the same wage

2. Assuming workers and jobs are identical, if information is perfect but job search and migration are costly, then:
    a.* labor may or may not flow among employers
    b. labor will flow among employers until all wages are equal
    c. labor will flow among employers until all economic profits are zero, but wages may be unequal
    d. all firms will hire the same number of workers in equilibrium and pay them all the same wage

Questions 3 and 4 refer to the following diagram:

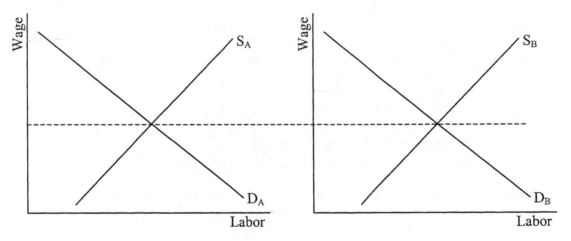

3. Consider the two labor markets shown in the diagram above. The wage rates shown represent:
    a. long run equilibrium
    b.* long run equilibrium if all nonwage aspects of the jobs are identical
    c. long run equilibrium provided the workers are in noncompeting groups
    d. long run equilibrium if information is perfect and costless

4. Suppose that all other nonwage aspects of the jobs in these two markets are identical. We would expect labor supply in B to increase if:
    a. the probability of job loss rises in B
    b.* earnings are more variable in A
    c. job safety improves in A
    d. there are better prospects for advancement in A

5. Which of the following is *not* a source of persistent compensating wage differentials?
   a.* migration from lower paying jobs to higher paying jobs
   b. fringe benefits
   c. job status
   d. different skill requirements

6. Suppose all workers are identical but working for Ajax is more pleasant than working for Acme. In all other nonwage respects the two firms offer the same job characteristics. In equilibrium:
   a. the wage at Ajax will be higher than at Acme
   b.* the wage at Ajax will be lower than at Acme
   c. workers will have lower net utility at Acme
   d. employment will be higher at Ajax if demand is the same in both markets

7. If job X pays more than identical job Y, then the wage rates will:
   a. remain different if mobility is costless
   b. remain different if information is perfect
   c. equalize because labor will migrate from X to Y
   d.* equalize if information is perfect and mobility is costless

8. The wage rate paid workers at Flow, Inc. will most likely exceed that at otherwise identical Stock Co. if:
   a. Flow, Inc. is a more prestigious firm than Stock Co.
   b. earnings are subject to greater variability at Stock, Co.
   c.* Stock Co. offers better pension and insurance benefits than Flow, Inc.
   d. the demand for labor at Stock Co. exceeds the demand for labor at Flow, Inc.

9. Compared to similar jobs, the wage paid to steelworkers in Youngstown, Ohio will be lower if:
   a.* the cost of living in Youngstown is lower than elsewhere
   b. working in the steel industry is more dangerous and loud
   c. steelworkers have less control over their work environment
   d. there are fewer prospects for promotion among steelworkers

10. Lower-paid workers often seem to have less desirable working conditions as well because:
    a. lower-paid workers tend to have proportionately greater fringe benefits.
    b. employers discriminate against unskilled workers
    c.* the compensating differential for skill often outweighs the compensating differential for poor working conditions
    d. the compensating differential for poor working conditions often outweighs the compensating differential for skill

11. People who receive relatively high pay also tend to work in a relatively desirable work environment. This is probably because:
    a. employers have imperfect information
    b. highly paid and poorly paid workers are in noncompeting groups
    c. firms with desirable working conditions are operating off their normal isoprofit curves
    d.* the differential required to compensate for high skill swamps the differential required for poor working conditions

Questions 12 and 13 refer to the diagram below, which represents a local labor market consisting of two submarkets. All workers are assumed to be identical.

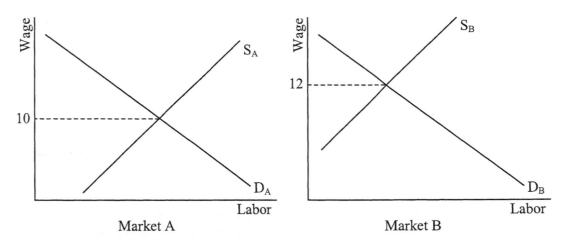

Market A   Market B

12. Assume that information is perfect, mobility between jobs is costless, and that all nonwage aspects of the two are identical. The outcome shown in the diagram:
a.   represents an equilibrium
b.   does not represent an equilibrium. The demand for labor in market A will shift rightward, and that in market B will shift leftward until wage rates equalize
c.* does not represent an equilibrium. The supply of labor in market A will shift leftward, and that in market B will shift rightward until the wage rates equalize
d.   does not represent an equilibrium. The supply of labor in market B will shift leftward, and that in market A will shift rightward until the wage rates equalize

13. Suppose that the wage in B is higher because workers perceive disutility of $2 associated with this job relative to A. Assuming that information is perfect and mobility between jobs is costless, we can conclude that:
a.* the wage differential between jobs A and B is an equilibrium differential
b.   workers will flow from job A to job B
c.   workers will flow from job B to job A
d.   the demand for labor in B will fall and the demand for labor in A will rise

14. Which one of the following is a *true* statement?
a.   Workers cannot ever move from one noncompeting group to another
b.* Wage differentials caused by the existence of noncompeting groups can persist over time
c.   The concept of noncompeting groups applies only to workers in different geographical locations; it does not apply to productivity differences among workers
d.   The concept of noncompeting groups explains why wage rates do not fall in a recession

15. Consider a worker who faces a tradeoff between job safety and wages. The less risk averse is the worker, the:
a.   lower is the wage earned by the worker
b.   steeper is this worker's indifference curves
c.* flatter is this worker's indifference curves
d.   lower are the profits of this worker's employer

Questions 16 – 18 refer to the following diagram.

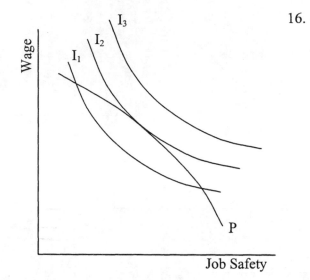

16. The shape of the worker's indifference curves—I_1, I_2, and I_3—indicates that:
    a.   the worker faces a constant trade-off between job safety and wages
    b.*   for each successive reduction in job safety, greater increases in wages are required to maintain the same utility
    c.   for each successive reduction in job safety, smaller increases in wages are required to maintain the same level of utility
    d.   for each successive reduction in job safety, smaller reductions in wages are required to maintain the same utility

17. The firm's isoprofit curve, P, is shown as concave to the origin, reflecting the assumption that:
    a.   the firm faces a constant trade-off between job safety and wages
    b.   each successive increase in job safety comes at a decreasing expense to the firm
    c.   each successive increase in job safety requires a smaller drop in wages to maintain normal profits
    d.*   each successive increase in job safety comes at an increasing expense to the firm

18. The highest level of utility the worker can possibly achieve is:
    a. I_1, if P is a normal-profit isoprofit curve
    b.* I_2, if P is a normal-profit isoprofit curve
    c. I_1, if P represents a positive economic profit
    d. I_3, if P is a normal-profit isoprofit curve

Questions 19 and 20 refer to the following diagram:

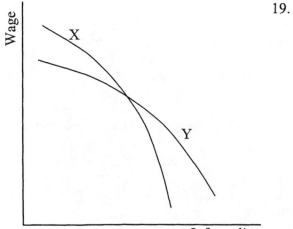

19. Consider a worker who faces a trade-off between higher wages and a more relaxed work environment as shown in the diagram. Relatively steep indifference curves indicate that the worker:
    a.*   places a relatively high value on additional informality on the job
    b.   will tend to work at a firm with a relatively informal environment, like firm X
    c.   will not willingly sacrifice informality for higher wages
    d.   does not place a relatively high value on additional informality on the job

20. Which one of the following best explains the differences in the isoprofit curves of the two firms?
    a.   X has lower profits than Y because X is paying higher wages
    b.   X has higher profits than Y because X's high wages attract workers who are less relaxed and thereby less likely to shirk on the job
    c.*   X pays a higher cost than Y for providing additional informality
    d.   Y pays a higher cost than X for providing additional informality

Questions 21 – 23 refer to the following diagrams:

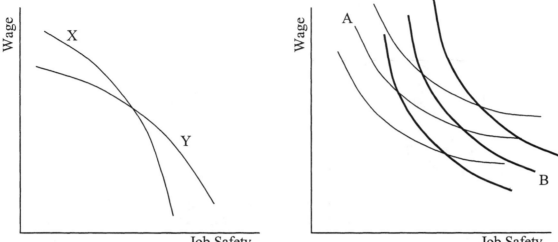

21. From the indifference curves, we can infer that worker A:
    a.   has a stronger taste for job safety relative to income than worker B
    b.   has the same taste for job safety relative to income than worker B
    c.*   has a stronger taste for income relative to job safety than worker B
    d.   has a lower skill level than worker B

22. In equilibrium:
    a.*   worker A will work for firm X; worker B will work for firm Y
    b.   worker A will work for firm Y; worker B will work for firm X
    c.   both workers will work for firm X
    d.   both workers will work for firm Y

23. As a result of the matching between workers and firms, firm X will pay:
    a.   a lower wage and provide less job safety than firm Y
    b.   a lower wage and provide more job safety than firm Y
    c.*   a higher wage and provide less job safety than firm Y
    d.   a higher wage and provide more job safety than firm Y

24. Which of the following is *not* predicted by the hedonic theory of wages, all else constant?
    a.   minimum safety standards do not necessarily benefit firms
    b.*   minimum safety standards benefit all workers
    c.   jobs that offer pleasant surroundings will pay less than those in which working conditions are poor
    d.   firms will tend to offer those fringe benefits that they can provide most cheaply

25. The hedonic theory of wages predicts that:
   a.   workers and firms will be matched randomly, but in equilibrium firms will be maximizing profits and workers will be maximizing utility
   b.   other things equal, workers who value job safety least will tend to work for firms that have the lowest cost of providing safe jobs
   c.*   other things equal, workers who value job safety least will tend to work for firms that have the highest cost of providing safe jobs
   d.   other things equal, workers who value job safety most will tend to work for firms that have the highest cost of providing safe jobs

26. Fringe benefit packages differ substantially from one firm to the next because:
   a.   labor market information is costless
   b.   adjustment periods tend to be short
   c.   worker mobility costs are low
   d.*   firms may structure their fringe benefit packages to attract specific types of workers

27. Imperfect and costly labor market information will likely result in:
   a.   wages converging to a common rate
   b.*   a distribution of wages around the mean for any occupation, independently of compensating differentials
   c.   an inverse relationship between wages and the risk of injury on the job
   d.   instantaneous adjustment to equilibrium in response to short-run wage differentials

28. An example of a sociological immobility is:
   a.   ties to family and friends prevent workers from moving to a region with relatively high wages
   b.   craft unions limit the access of nonunion workers to apprenticeship positions
   c.   state governments require workers in many jobs to obtain a license
   d.*   the so-called "glass ceiling" (a form of discrimination) prevents women from moving into certain high-paying managerial jobs

29. "The high psychic costs of leaving friends and family deter migration in response to wage differentials." This statement reflects the existence of:
   a.*   geographic immobilities   c.   institutional immobilities
   b.   sociological immobilities   d.   wage immobilities

30. (*World of Work* 8-1) Research by Krueger and Allen suggests that a substantial proportion of the increase in the college wage premium in the 1980s can be explained by:
   a.   increased college enrollment by men
   b.   increased college enrollment by women
   c.   increased immigration rates
   d.*   skill-biased technological change

31. (*World of Work* 8-2) Compared to nonsmokers, smokers' wages tend to be:
   a.   higher because they are more relaxed on the job and are absent less often
   b.   higher because they are more productive workers
   c.*   lower because they have higher costs associated with absenteeism, insurance, and low morale
   d.   lower because their unemployment rate is higher

32. (*World of Work* 8-3) If men expecting to be married also expect to work more hours, then on average:
   - a.* married men will have more education and higher wages than single men
   - b. wages of married and single men will converge over time
   - c. married men will find that financing education is more costly than for single men
   - d. married men will have lower wages but higher earnings than single men

33. (*World of Work* 8-4) According to recent research by Kostiuk, "shift work":
   - a. is relatively rare because such workers do not earn a compensating wage differential
   - b. is more common than generally understood because such workers do not earn a compensating wage differential
   - c. provides a greater wage premium for highly educated workers than for less educated workers
   - d.* provides a greater wage premium for less educated workers than for highly educated workers

34. (*World of Work* 8-5) The hedonic method of valuing a human life:
   - a.* is based on the information inherent in compensating wage differentials
   - b. estimates the present value of the amount of wage and fringe benefits that would have been made had the worker not been killed
   - c. typically results in a value of between $500,000 and $700,000 per life lost
   - d. typically yields lower estimates than does the human capital approach

CHAPTER 9
Mobility, Migration, and Efficiency

I.   TYPES OF LABOR MOBILITY
    A.   Box I: Job Change/No Change in Occupation or Residence
    B.   Box II: Occupational Change/No Change in Residence
    C.   Box III: Geographic Change/No Change in Occupation
    D.   Box IV: Geographic Change/Change in Occupation

II.   MIGRATION AS AN INVESTMENT IN HUMAN CAPITAL

III.   THE DETERMINANTS OF MIGRATION: A CLOSER LOOK
    A.   Age
    B.   Family Factors
    C.   Education
    D.   Distance
    E.   Unemployment Rates
    F.   Other Factors

IV.   THE CONSEQUENCES OF MIGRATION
    A.   Personal Gains
        1.   Empirical Evidence
        2.   Caveats
            a.   Uncertainty and Imperfect Information
            b.   Timing of Earnings Gains
            c.   Earnings Disparities
            d.   Earnings of Spouses
            e.   Wage Reductions from Job Losses
    B.   Wage Narrowing and Efficiency Gains
        1.   Numerical Illustration
        2.   Graphic Portrayal
    C.   External effects
        1.   Real Negative Externalities
        2.   Pecuniary Externalities: Income Redistribution
            a.   Losses in the Origin Nation
            b.   Reduced Wage Income to Native Workers
            c.   Gains to Owners of Capital
            d.   Fiscal Impacts

V.   CAPITAL AND PRODUCT FLOWS
    A.   Capital Flows
    B.   Product Flows

VI.   U.S. IMMIGRATION POLICY AND ISSUES
    A.   History and Scope
    B.   Effects of Illegal Immigration
        1.   Employment Effects
        2.   Wage Effects
        3.   Fiscal Effects

WORLD OF WORK
1.   Determinants of Occupational Tenure
2.   The Mexican *Maquiladoras*

GLOBAL PERSPECTIVE
1.   Immigrants as a Percent of the Population, 1991 – 1993

LEARNING OBJECTIVES

After learning the material in Chapter 9 of *Contemporary Labor Economics*, the student should be able to:

1.   distinguish between the various types of labor mobility and explain the relative importance of each

2.   identify and detail the costs and benefits of labor migration

3.   use the analytical framework of human capital investment to explain the migration decision of a household

4.   list the determinants of migration

5.   state the formula for V_p, the present value of net benefits from mobility, and use it to predict the impacts of the various determinants of mobility

6.   describe the economic consequences of labor migration

7.   explain why, on average, the long-term wage gains of migrants tend to exceed the short-term wage gains

8.   graphically illustrate the efficiency gains from migration

9.   distinguish the personal costs and benefits of mobility from any possible external costs and benefits, whether real or pecuniary

10. explain how capital and product flows affect wage differentials and labor mobility

11. identify specific groups of gainers and losers from migration in both the origin and destination

12. describe the history and scope of U.S. immigration policy, including current policy

13. explain recent evidence on legal and illegal immigration

14. critically evaluate the economic impact of illegal aliens

ANSWERS TO SELECTED END-OF-CHAPTER QUESTIONS

1.   Increases in age, distance, and the discount rate will likely reduce the net present value of migration. V_p is also likely to be smaller for married persons: gains for one spouse may result in losses for the other. The foregone earnings of the move will also be higher if both spouses are employed. Increased education will likely increase the net gains from migration.

4.   a.   Combined output rises.
     b.   Capital income rises and labor income falls in the destination.
     c.   The average wage rate rises in the origin.
     d.   The total wage bill for natives falls in the destination.

70

8.   Monopsony implies workers have restricted geographic or occupational choice. Mobility increases the choices they have available and thereby makes their labor supply curves to any given firm more elastic.

MULTIPLE CHOICE QUESTIONS

1.   Linda quit her job as a loan officer at First Detroit State Bank to accept a similar position at First Minneapolis Savings Bank. This is an example of:
a.*   geographic mobility   c.   horizontal mobility
b.   occupational mobility   d.   vertical mobility

2.   If an economics professor moves from the University of California at Berkeley to the University of Texas at Austin, that is an example of:
a.   job change/no change in residence
b.   occupational change/no change in residence
c.*   geographic change/no change in occupation
d.   geographic change/change in occupation

3.   Because migration typically involves present sacrifice in order to obtain a greater stream of future earnings, many economists consider migration to be:
a.*   an investment in human capital
b.   undertaken only by those who have very low discount rates
c.   motivated strictly by monetary considerations
d.   an impediment to economic efficiency

4.   All else equal, a worker is less likely to move:
a.*   the smaller the wage differential between the destination and the origin
b.   the lower the discount rate
c.   the greater the number of years one expects to remain in the new location
d.   the lower the indirect costs of migrating

5.   All else equal, a worker is more likely to move if:
a.   the spouse is also a labor force participant
b.   there are school-age children in the family
c.*   the spouse has accumulated very little job tenure
d.   he or she is married

6.   All else equal, a worker is less likely to move:
a.   if the worker has moved before
b.*   the greater the amount of specific training the worker has
c.   the greater the worker's educational attainment
d.   the shorter the distance moved

7.   All else equal, a worker is more likely to move:
a.   the greater the wage differential between the destination and the origin
b.   the greater the direct costs of moving
c.   the larger the worker's family size
d.*   the lower the discount rate

71

8.	All else equal, a worker is less likely to move:
	a.	if he or she has moved before
	b.*	the more unionized the worker's occupation
	c.	the greater the worker's educational attainment
	d.	if the worker is single

9.	Which one of the following helps to explain the observed relationship between age and mobility?
	a.*	Older workers tend to have more specific human capital and on-the-job training
	b.	Older workers tend to have more general training
	c.	Younger workers have less time to recoup their investment costs
	d.	Both direct and psychic costs of moving tend to decrease with age.

10.	Which one of the following will tend to decrease the perceived costs of a move relative to the perceived benefits?
	a.*	Renting, as opposed to owning, one's home
	b.	An increase in the unemployment rate in the destination
	c.	Larger family size
	d.	Increased federal grants and defense contracts in the origin

11.	The average economic rate of return to migration is estimated to be:
	a.	negative	c.*	between 10% and 15%
	b.	between 0% and 5%	d.	between 20% and 25%

12.	The expected private rate of return to migration to a particular individual:
	a.*	is similar to that on other forms of investment in human capital
	b.	equals that individual's actual rate of return
	c.	cannot be determined because there are backflows in migration
	d.	cannot be determined because there are earnings disparities between the origin and the destination

13.	Early empirical evidence reported by Barry Chiswick indicates that foreign-born persons migrating to the U.S., all else constant:
	a.	tend to earn more than natives from the time they arrive at the destination
	b.*	initially tend to earn less than natives, catch up after 10-15 years, and eventually surpass natives
	c.	typically do not catch up to the earnings of native-born workers, even after several years
	d.	have little or no variance in their earnings

14.	Research by Borjas on relatively recent immigrants to the U.S. suggests that they:
	a.	tend to earn more than natives from the time they arrive at the destination
	b.	initially tend to earn less than natives, catch up after 10-15 years, and eventually surpass natives
	c.	have little or no variance in their earnings
	d.*	typically do not catch up to the earnings of native-born workers, even after several years

15.	Assuming competitive markets, migration in response to wage differentials will likely result in:
	a.	an increase in the total value of output, but reduced economic efficiency
	b.	a decrease in both the value of output and economic efficiency
	c.*	an increase in both the value of output and economic efficiency
	d.	an increase in the size of the wage differential

Questions 16 and 17 refer to the following information. There are initially 28 workers in market A and 63 workers in market B. All markets are assumed competitive; A and B are identical in all nonwage aspects.

L_A	VMP_A	L_B	VMP_B
25	10.00	60	12.00
26	9.50	61	11.50
27	9.00	62	11.00
28	8.50	63	10.50
29	8.00	64	10.00
30	7.50	65	9.50
31	7.00	66	9.00

16. Given the initial situation (assuming perfect information and costless migration) which one of the following may be expected to occur?
    a.* Workers will migrate from A to B
    b. Workers will migrate from B to A
    c. There will be no migration of workers
    d. A migration pattern cannot be determined from the information

17. After all adjustments to equilibrium take place in this market, we expect to find that:
    a. the total value of output is increased, but economic efficiency is reduced
    b.* both the total value of output and economic efficiency are increased
    c. both the total value of output and economic efficiency are reduced
    d. changes in the total value of output and economic efficiency cannot be determined

Questions 18 – 20 refer to the following diagram. Suppose initially that wage rates are W_M in Country M and W_U in Country U. Further suppose that migration results in an equalization of wage rates.

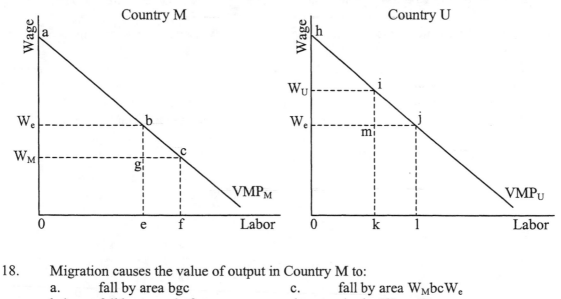

18. Migration causes the value of output in Country M to:
    a. fall by area bgc   c. fall by area $W_M$bcW_e
    b.* fall by area ebcf   d. rise by $W_M - W_e$

19. Migration causes a collective loss to Country U workers equal to area:
    a. imj   c.* $W_U$imW_e
    b. kijl   d. $W_U$ijW_e

20. Migration causes a collective loss to Country M capital owners equal to area:
    a. bgc
    c. $0W_ebe$
    b. ebcf
    d.* W_ebcW_M

21. Suppose a proposed law will ban migration into the U.S.. Considering who gains and who loses from migration, economic theory suggests that, in general:
    a. U.S. businesses and U.S. workers would support the law
    b. U.S. businesses and U.S. workers would object to the law
    c. U.S. businesses would support the law while U.S. workers would object to it
    d.* U.S. businesses would object to the law and U.S. workers would support it

22. Suppose a proposed law will expand migration into the U.S.. Considering who gains and who loses from migration, economic theory suggests that there will be a net gain accruing to U.S. workers who are:
    a. gross substitutes with new immigrants
    b.* gross complements with new immigrants
    c. employed in the same market as new immigrants
    d. employed in exporting industries

23. The total net private gain from migration to migrants and their employers:
    a. is the increase in annual wages resulting from migration
    b. tends to overstate the social gain if there are real external benefits associated with the move
    c.* tends to overstate the social gain if there are real external costs associated with the move
    d. tends to understate the social gain if there are pecuniary external costs associated with the move

24. Which of the following would be considered a real (not a pecuniary) externality associated with migration?
    a. Capital owners in the origin will lose income as wages rise in response to reduced labor supply
    b.* More public services will be required in the destination and there will be excess capacity of public goods in the origin
    c. Profits of capital owners at the origin will rise as migrants leave
    d. Wages of destination workers will fall as migrants enter and add to labor supply

Answer questions 25 – 28 on the basis of the following diagram. Assume all migration is costless.

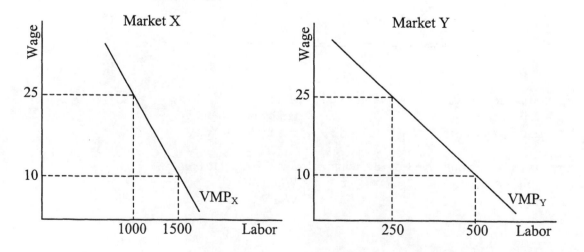

25. If there are initially 1000 workers in country X and 500 workers in country Y, then we should expect:
    a.   net migration from country X to country Y
    b.* net migration from country Y to country X
    c.   There will be no migration of workers
    d.   A migration pattern cannot be determined from the information

26. Assume there are initially 1000 workers in country X and 500 workers in country Y. Once equilibrium has been established the total value of output will:
    a.* have increased in country X and decreased in country Y; the combined total has increased
    b.   have increased in country X and decreased in country Y; the combined total has decreased
    c.   have increased in country X and decreased in country Y; the combined total has not changed
    d.   not change

27. If wages are initially $10 in country X and $25 in country Y, then we should expect higher rates of capital investment in:
    a.* X relative to Y, eventually resulting in increased labor demand in X
    b.   X relative to Y, eventually resulting in reduced labor demand in X
    c.   Y relative to X, eventually resulting in increased labor demand in X
    d.   Y relative to X, eventually resulting in reduced labor demand in X

28. If wages are initially $10 in country X and $25 in country Y, then we should expect a relative price advantage in country:
    a.* X, eventually resulting in greater export sales to Y and thus greater derived demand for labor in X
    b.   Y, eventually resulting in greater export sales to X and thus greater derived demand for labor in Y
    c.   X, eventually resulting in greater imports from Y thus greater derived demand for labor in X
    d.   Y, eventually resulting in greater imports from X and thus greater derived demand for labor in Y

29. Historically, immigrants in the U.S.A.:
    a.   have been less likely than the native-born population to receive welfare benefits and welfare participation by immigrants has not changed in recent years
    b.* have been less likely than the native-born population to receive welfare benefits but welfare participation by immigrants has increased in recent years
    c.   have been more likely than the native-born population to receive welfare benefits and welfare participation by immigrants has not changed in recent years
    d.   have been more likely than the native-born population to receive welfare benefits but welfare participation by immigrants has decreased in recent years

30. Legal immigration to the U.S.:
    a.   peaked early in the twentieth century
    b.   typically is less than illegal immigration
    c.   is heavily skewed towards northern and western European nations by law
    d.* is biased in favor of relatives of U.S. citizens and people who have specific job skills

31.   Estimates by the U.S. Bureau of the Census suggest that total legal and illegal immigration to the U.S. each year is approximately:
a.   300,000 persons   c.   4,000,000 persons
b.*   1,000,000 persons   d.   12,000,000 persons

32.   Immigration to the United States:
a.   peaked in the 1920s with a strong wave of northern Europeans
b.   was less in 1980 than 1970
c.   increased between 1980 and 1985 but then fell off in the later 1980s
d.*   surged in the early 1990s because of the amnesty provisions in the Immigration Reform and Control Act

33.   An increase of 500 illegal alien workers would most likely:
a.   increase domestic unemployment by 500
b.   increase wages paid to native workers in industries which typically hire illegal aliens, attracting less than 500 native workers into these jobs
c.   reduce wages paid to native workers in industries which typically hire illegal aliens, displacing more than 500 native workers from these jobs
d.*   reduce wages paid to native workers in industries which typically hire illegal aliens, displacing less than 500 native workers from these jobs

34.   Suppose there is an increase in immigration rates of unskilled, illegal aliens. Which of the following is *not* likely to result:
a.   Unskilled workers would lose if they are gross substitutes with illegal immigrants
b.   Skilled workers would benefit if they are gross complements with unskilled workers
c.   The wages of unskilled workers would fall in those markets not protected by minimum wages
d.*   For each immigrant who receives a job there would be one less job available for a native worker

35.   (*World of Work* 9-1) Occupational tenure tends to be highest for:
a.*   self-employed, men, and those with a college education
b.   self-employed, women, and those with no more than a high school education
c.   workers in large firms, women, and those with a college education
d.   workers in small firms, men, and those with no more than a high school education

36.   (*World of Work* 9-2) By liberalizing the flow of capital and goods throughout North America, NAFTA eventually would:
a.   encourage the development of *maquiladoras*
b.*   reduce the need for *maquiladoras*
c.   have no impact on the future development of *maquiladoras*
d.   have no impact on current *maquiladoras* because they are quasi-fixed resources

CHAPTER 10
Labor Unions and Collective Bargaining

I.   WHY UNIONS?

II.   LABOR UNIONISM: FACTS AND FIGURES
      A.   Who Belongs to Unions?
            1.   Industry and Occupation
            2.   Personal Characteristics: Gender, Race, and Age
            3.   Location
      B.   Structure of Organized Labor
            1.   AFL-CIO
            2.   National Unions
            3.   Local Unions
            4.   Diversity of Bargaining Structures

III. UNIONISM'S DECLINE
      A.   Structural Changes
      B.   Managerial-Opposition Hypothesis
      C.   The Substitution Hypothesis
      D.   Other Factors
      E.   Relative Importance
      F.   Union Responses
            1.   Mergers
            2.   Changes in Strategies

IV.   ARE UNIONS MAXIMIZERS?
      A.   Economic Models
            1.   Wage Rate
            2.   Wage Bill
            3.   Employment and Membership
      B.   Political Models
      C.   Synopsis

V.   COLLECTIVE BARGAINING: A COMPLEX TRANSACTION
      A.   Delivering Labor Services
      B.   Long-Term Relationship
      C.   Negotiations

VI.   A MODEL OF THE BARGAINING PROCESS
      A.   The Model
      B.   Implications
            1.   Requirement for Agreement
            2.   Relative Bargaining Power
            3.   "Unnecessary" Strikes
                  a.   Misjudgment
                  b.   Commitments
            4.   Reaching Agreement

5.   Negotiating Tactics: Coercion and Persuasion
      a.   Coercive Tactics
      b.   Persuasive Tactics
6.   The Economic Environment
      a.   Prosperity and Recession
      b.   Industry Structure

WORLD OF WORK
1.   Should the Right to Hire Permanent Strikebreakers be Rescinded?
2.   Revitalization of Unions?
3.   Unionism's Decline: Unique to the United States?
4.   And Finally the Contract was Signed!

GLOBAL PERSPECTIVE
1.   Union Membership as a Percent of the Employed Workers, 1987 – 1989

LEARNING OBJECTIVES

After learning the material in Chapter 10 of *Contemporary Labor Economics*, the student should be able to:

1.   describe the historical background to the development of labor unions

2.   describe the distribution of union membership by industry, occupation, geographical location, age, race, and gender

3.   cite the reasons for the growth of public sector unionism in the 1960s and 1970s, despite the decline in private sector unionism

4.   outline the basic structure of American labor unionism, noting the relationships between union federations, national unions, and local unions

5.   distinguish between the terms "bargaining structure," "master agreement," "pattern bargaining," and "multi-employer bargaining"

6.   explain how and why bargaining structures vary by industry

7.   summarize recent trends in private sector unionism and evaluate the various explanations for the relative decline in union membership since the 1950s and the absolute decline in the 1980s

8.   describe strategies unions have used to stem the decline in their membership

9.   explain and illustrate why a union's objective is not always obvious

10.   explain the ways in which collective bargaining differs from other types of transactions

11.   define "bargaining power" and show how this concept relates to the costs of agreeing and disagreeing in bargaining

12.   list several factors that will increase a union's or a firm's bargaining power

13.   distinguish between the necessary and sufficient conditions for a wage settlement in the Chamberlain bargaining power model

14.   explain the difference between coercive and persuasive bargaining tactics and list examples of each

ANSWERS TO SELECTED END-OF-CHAPTER QUESTIONS

4.   Statements (a) and (b) reflect the "structural change" hypothesis. Statement (c) reflects the "managerial opposition" hypothesis.

5.   Contributing factors to the rapid growth of public sector unionism in the 1960s and 1970s include:
     1.   at state and local levels, laws that allowed government workers to unionize and required government employers to bargain with their unions;
     2.   at the federal level, executive orders that encouraged unionization.

     Other factors may include a "pent-up" demand by government workers for unions and relatively little resistance to unions by government employers.

10.   Statements (a) – (d) illustrate coercive tactics. Statements (e) – (g) illustrate persuasive tactics.

MULTIPLE CHOICE QUESTIONS

1.   The authors suggest that unions developed primarily in response to:
     a.   purposeful mistreatment by employers
     b.   the inability of preindustrial workers to be self-sufficient
     c.*   dependency of workers on factory owners as a result of industrialization
     d.   attempts by employers to achieve an eight-hour day

2.   Approximately what percentage of U.S. workers were union members in 1996?
     a.   8%   b.*   14%   c.   22%   d.   31%

3.   Of the countries listed in the text, union membership as a percent of the labor force is greatest in:
     a.   the United States   c.   Canada
     b.   Japan   d.*   Sweden

4.   Which one of the following is generally *not* associated with relatively high levels of unionization?
     a.*   Service industries   c.   Blacks
     b.   Public administration   d.   Blue-collar workers

5.   As of 1996, which of the following U.S. industries was less than 15% unionized?
     a.   transportation, communication, and public utilities
     b.   public administration
     c.*   wholesale and retail trade
     d.   construction

6.   As of 1996, which of the following U.S. industries was more than 30% unionized?
     a.   mining   c.   wholesale and retail trade
     b.   construction   d.*   public administration

7.   White-collar workers:
     a.   are just as likely as blue-collar workers to be union members
     b.*   are less likely to unionize because unionization may be an obstacle to their ambitions
     c.   are more likely to unionize because the potential gains from unionization are larger
     d.   are exempt from most labor legislation

8.   Unions are most prevalent in the:
      a.*   urban north   c.   urban south
      b.   nonindustrial southwest   d.   suburban east

9.   In which industry is the relatively high extent of unionism and union membership growth
      explained by the favorable legislative climate of the 1960s and 1970s?
      a.   Finance, insurance and real estate
      b.   Wholesale and retail trade
      c.   Transportation, communication and public utilities
      d.*   Public Administration

10.   The largest labor union in the U.S. is the:
      a.   United Steelworkers   c.   Brotherhood of Teamsters
      b.   United Rubber Workers   d.*   National Education Association

11.   An example of a union federation is the:
      a.   American Medical Association   c.   United Auto Workers
      b.   Air Line Pilots Association   d.*   AFL-CIO

12.   The level of union organization that is most likely to lobby congress for legislation that prohibits
      the hiring of permanent strikebreakers is the:
      a.*   federation   c.   national union
      b.   state union   d.   local union

13.   The level of union organization that is most likely to negotiate a collective bargaining agreement
      is the:
      a.   federation   c.   state union
      b.*   national union   d.   local union

14.   Which of the following is *not* a major responsibility of a national union?
      a.   organizing workers in its craft or industry
      b.   negotiating collective bargaining agreements
      c.*   handling grievance procedures
      d.   settling jurisdictional disputes

15.   The local union has primary responsibility for:
      a.   organizing workers in its craft or industry
      b.   negotiating collective bargaining agreements
      c.*   handling grievance procedures
      d.   settling jurisdictional disputes

16.   Negotiating a contract with a group of firms in an industry is an example of:
      a.   pattern bargaining   c.   coercive bargaining
      b.   collective bargaining   d.*   multiemployer bargaining

17.   Compared to the 1950s, current union membership as a percent of the labor force in the U.S. is:
      a.   the same in the private sector and higher in the public sector
      b.*   lower in the private sector and higher in the public sector
      c.   the same in the private sector and lower in the public sector
      d.   lower in the private sector and lower in the public sector

18. Union membership as a percentage of the labor force in the U.S.:
   a. peaked in the 1920s
   b. has fallen since the 1960s, although the absolute number of union members has continuously increased
   c.* has fallen since the 1960s, including a decline in the absolute number of union members in the 1980s and 1990s
   d. increased steadily since the 1880s

19. Which one of the following hypotheses is *not* generally given as an explanation of the change in relative union membership?
   a. managerial-opposition hypothesis   c. structural-change hypothesis
   b.* union-growth hypothesis   d. substitution hypothesis

20. "The industry mix of national output has changed from manufacturing to services, resulting in a relative decline in union membership." This argument is most consistent with the:
   a. managerial-opposition hypothesis   c.* structural-change hypothesis
   b. union-growth hypothesis   d. substitution hypothesis

21. Over the last few decades the composition of the labor force has changed to include a greater proportion of women and younger workers. This fact is most consistent with the:
   a. managerial-opposition hypothesis   c.* structural-change hypothesis
   b. union-growth hypothesis   d. substitution hypothesis

22. According to research by Neumann and Rissman, many government programs provide "union-like" services, which has contributed to the decline of unionization. Their findings illustrate the:
   a. managerial-opposition hypothesis   c. structural-change hypothesis
   b. union-growth hypothesis   d.* substitution hypothesis

23. Studies by Farber and by Freeman and Medoff have suggested that:
   a. managerial opposition has been steady over the years, and has not contributed to the decline of unionization
   b.* about 40% of unions' decline can be explained by structural changes in the economy
   c. shrinking union wage premiums have made it easy for firms to employ anti-union tactics
   d. recent NLRB rulings have been increasingly favorable to unions and should stop the decline in their membership

24. In response to declines in membership, unions have recently:
   a. avoided labor organization mergers
   b. intensified attempts to organize blue-collar workers as opposed to white-collar workers
   c. given increased priority to wage increases and put less emphasis on leaves for child care and flexible work schedules
   d.* substituted work slowdowns for strikes as a way of preventing replacement by permanent strikebreakers

Questions 25 – 27 refer to the information in the following table. Q_s and Q_d are the quantities of labor supplied and demanded, respectively:

Wage	Q_s	Q_d
$ 6	16	36
8	22	32
10	28	28
12	34	24
14	40	20
16	46	16

25. If the union wishes to maximize its membership and employment, it would set a wage rate of:
   a. $6   c. $12
   b.* $10   d. $16

26. To maximize the wage bill, the union would set a wage of:
   a. $6   c.* $12
   b. $10   d. $16

27. If the labor market is initially in equilibrium, and the union sets a wage of $14, employment will:
   a.*   fall by 8   c.   fall by 4
   b.   rise by 12   d.   not be affected

Questions 28 and 29 refer to the following diagram:

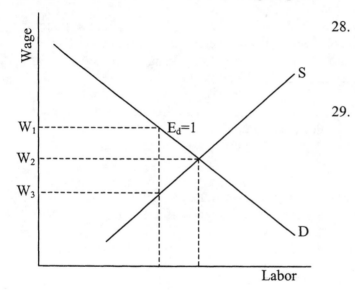

28. Suppose that the union wishes to maximize the wage bill. It should bargain for wage:
   a.* W_1 c. W_3
   b. W_2 d.   above W_1

29. Which wage would maximize the union's membership and employment?
   a. W_1 c. W_3
   b.* W_2 d.   above W_1

30. In contrast to the typical product-market transaction, collective bargaining:
   a.   reflects the short-term relationship between buyer and seller
   b.*   involves negotiation between buyer and seller
   c.   ignores the conditions under which the sale takes place
   d.   is subject to market power on the side of the buyer, rather than the seller

31. Typically, collective bargaining negotiations:
   a.   only involve wage determination
   b.   determine the prices firms charge in the sale of their output
   c.*   focus on issues in addition to wage determination, such as company operations, promotion policies, and training
   d.   are conducted on a "take-it-or leave-it" basis

32. In Chamberlain's model, management's bargaining power is:
   a.   management's cost of agreeing divided by management's cost of disagreeing
   b.   management's cost of disagreeing divided by management's cost of agreeing
   c.   the union's cost of agreeing divided by the union's cost of disagreeing
   d.*   the union's cost of disagreeing divided by the union's cost of agreeing

33. In Chamberlain's model, which of the following will increase management's bargaining power?
   a.   An increase in the union's perceived cost of agreeing with management's terms
   b.*   An increase in the union's perceived cost of disagreeing with management's terms
   c.   The union sponsors a study showing how higher wages result in increased productivity
   d.   The union pickets the plant gate

34. According to Chamberlain's model, a necessary condition for agreement to a wage dispute is that:
   a.   both union and management bargaining power are less than one
   b.   both union and management bargaining power are equal to one
   c.*   at least one party's bargaining power is greater than one
   d.   at least one party's bargaining power is less than one

35. An example of a coercive bargaining tactic employed by the union is:
   a.   a lockout
   b.   a union study that concludes that higher wages increase worker productivity
   c.   the employment of permanent strikebreakers
   d.*   a strike vote

36. Which of the following will have an ambiguous effect on management's bargaining power? Management:
   a.   threatens a lockout
   b.*   increases its latest compensation offer
   c.   builds up its inventories during early stages of the negotiations
   d.   places an advertisement in the paper outlining the reasonableness of its position

37. According to Chamberlain's model, if the necessary condition for agreement to a wage dispute is satisfied, then:
   a.   a strike will not occur
   b.*   a strike still may occur
   c.   a strike will occur
   d.   a strike will only occur if neither party makes any misjudgments or irreversible commitments

38. A union's bargaining power will most likely increase if:
   a.*   its strike fund, which makes payments to union members during a strike, has just been enriched
   b.   its strike fund, which makes payments to union members during a strike, has just been depleted
   c.   management has just purchased strike insurance, which will make payments to the firm to replace lost profits if there is a strike
   d.   management threatens a lockout

39. Management is using a persuasive tactic if it:
    a. threatens to reduce contributions to the worker's pension funds
    b. promises a lockout should no agreement be reached by the deadline
    c. reduces its inventories during negotiations
    d.* states that lower wages would allow the firm to lower its prices and increase its market share, thereby expanding employment opportunities for union workers

40. A compromise wage offered by the firm in the direction of the union's wage demand will:
    a. increase the firm's cost of disagreeing, thus increasing its bargaining power
    b. decrease the firm's cost of disagreeing, thus increasing its bargaining power
    c. decrease the union's cost of disagreeing, thus increasing management's bargaining power
    d.* decrease the union's cost of agreeing *and* the firm's cost of disagreeing, thus having an uncertain effect on management's bargaining power

41. As the economy expands:
    a. both the union's and management's bargaining power increase
    b. both the union's and management's bargaining power decrease
    c.* the union's bargaining power increases and management's power decreases
    d. the union's bargaining power decreases and management's power increases

42. (*World of Work* 10-1) If employers are prohibited form hiring permanent strikebreakers:
    a. union bargaining power will likely fall
    b. management bargaining power will likely increase
    c. firms will only have one alternative under labor law—to fire strikers
    d.* the number of strikes will likely increase

43. (*World of Work* 10-2) One promising tactic unions have employed to stem the decline in union membership is:
    a.* devoting more resources to getting new members
    b. devoting more resources to political causes
    c. focusing organizing drives on relatively high-wage workers where unions are traditionally weak
    d. focusing organizing drives on women and minorities in professional organizations

44. (*World of Work* 10-3) Leo Troy presented evidence that private sector unionism declined in Canada even though overall union membership increased. He further showed that the shift from manufacturing to services there began later and proceeded more slowly than in the United States. This evidence supports the:
    a. unionism decline hypothesis   c. substitution hypothesis
    b. managerial opposition hypothesis   d.* structural change hypothesis

CHAPTER 11
The Economic Impact of Unions

I. THE UNION WAGE ADVANTAGE
    A.   Preliminary Complications
    B.   Measuring the Wage Advantage
          1.   Spillover Effects
          2.   Threat Effect
          3.   Other Effects
    C.   Empirical Evidence
    D.   Total Compensation: Wages plus Fringe benefits
          1.   Evidence
          2.   Role of Unions

II. EFFICIENCY AND PRODUCTIVITY
    A.   Negative View
          1.   Restrictive Work Rules
          2.   Strikes
          3.   Wage Advantage and Labor Misallocation
               a.   A Simple Model
               b.   Qualifications
                    (1)   Unemployment
                    (2)   Job Search Costs
                    (3)   Bilateral Monopoly
                    (4)   Investment Behavior and Productivity Growth
          4.   Empirical Estimates
    B.   Positive View
          1.   Investment and Technological Progress
          2.   Unions as a Collective Voice
                a.   The Voice Mechanism
                b.   Reduced Turnover
                c.   Seniority and Informal Training
                d.   Managerial Performance
    C.   Mixed Empirical Evidence

III. FIRM PROFITABILITY

IV. DISTRIBUTION OF EARNINGS
    A.   Increasing Inequality
          1.   Union-Nonunion Wages
          2.   Blue-Collar Wages
          3.   Skilled Labor Demand
    B.   Promoting Equality
          1.   Uniform Wages within Firms
          2.   Uniform Wages among Firms
          3.   Reducing the White-Collar to Blue-Collar Differential
    C.   Increased Equality?

V. OTHER ISSUES: INFLATION, UNEMPLOYMENT, AND INCOME SHARES
    A. Inflation
    B. Unions and Unemployment
    C. Labor's Share

WORLD OF WORK
    1. Two-Tier Wage Systems
    2. The Effect of International Competition on the Union Wage Advantage
    3. The Impact of a Strike on Other Workers
    4. The Effects of Teacher Unions on Productivity

GLOBAL PERSPECTIVE
    1. Strike Incidence, 1991 – 1995

LEARNING OBJECTIVES

After learning the material in Chapter 11 of *Contemporary Labor Economics*, the student should be able to:

1. define and use correctly the terms "spillover effect," "threat effect," "product-market effect," and "superior-worker effect"

2. compute the union wage advantage and state its significance

3. list several complications that arise in the measurement of the pure union wage advantage; for each determine whether the measured advantage will over- or understate the pure advantage

4. summarize the findings of empirical research on the extent of the union wage advantage

5. cite variations in the union wage advantage by industry, occupation, race, gender, and the state of the economy

6. explain why unionized workers generally receive more generous fringe benefits than nonunionized workers

7. graphically identify the efficiency loss caused by the spillover effect

8. list and explain the ways by which unions may affect productivity and allocative efficiency

9. describe the effects of unionism on firm profitability

10. describe how unions may either decrease or increase the inequality of earnings

11. assess the impact of unions on inflation, employment, unemployment, and the share of national income paid as wages

ANSWERS TO SELECTED END-OF-CHAPTER QUESTIONS

3. The pure union wage advantage is the percentage by which the union wage exceeds the wage that would prevail without the union. In the example, the pure union wage advantage is 25%.

    The measured union wage advantage will be biased upward in examples (a) and (d); it will be biased downward in examples (b) and (c).

4.	Approximately 18%. The advantage peaked in the mid 1970s but has been fairly steady for the past decade. The union wage advantage appears to be countercyclical.

9.	a.	Union demand curves will be less elastic, nonunion demand curves more elastic.
	b.	Holding the wage gain constant, the efficiency loss will be smaller.

MULTIPLE CHOICE QUESTIONS

1.	A union wage advantage is *less* likely to occur where:
	a.	the "spillover effect" outweighs the "threat effect"
	b.	product markets are characterized by substantial monopoly power
	c.*	only a few firms within a competitive industry are unionized
	d.	there is a distinct "shock effect"

2.	If union workers in a given occupation are paid $20 per hour while nonunion workers receive $16 per hour, the measured union wage advantage is:
	a.	20%	c.	80%
	b.*	25%	d.	more information is required

3.	If nonunion workers in a given occupation are paid $16 per hour while union workers receive $20 per hour, the pure union wage advantage is:
	a.	20%	c.	80%
	b.	25%	d.*	more information is required

4.	The nonunion wage rate may fall as the result of a union wage increase because of the:
	a.	product-market effect	c.	threat effect
	b.*	spillover effect	d.	compensating wage differential effect

5.	The nonunion wage rate may rise as the result of a union wage increase because of the:
	a.	spillover effect	c.*	threat effect
	b.	superior-worker effect	d.	compensating wage differential effect

6.	Suppose the union wage rate rises. The "spillover effect" suggests that the nonunion wage rate should _____; the "threat effect" suggests that the nonunion wage rate should _____.
	a.	fall, fall	c.*	fall, rise
	b.	rise, fall	d.	rise, rise

7.	"The union wage advantage is understated because nonunion wages rise as consumer demand shifts away from relatively higher priced union produced goods." This describes the:
	a.*	product-market effect	c.	superior-worker effect
	b.	spillover effect	d.	threat effect

8.	The measured union wage advantage will *understate* the pure advantage because of the:
	a.	spillover effect	c.*	product market effect
	b.	superior-worker effect	d.	compensating wage differential effect

Questions 9 – 11 refer to the following diagram. Wages in both the union and nonunion sectors are initially $10. The union negotiates a wage rate of $12. The post-negotiation wage is as yet unknown in the nonunion sector.

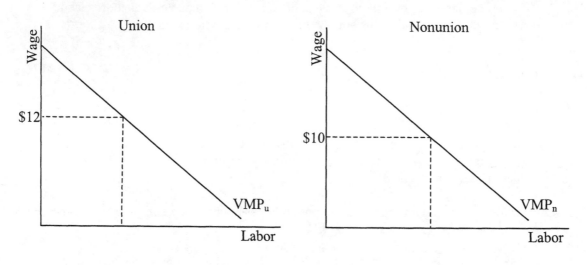

9. The measured union wage advantage in this market is:
   a. 20%
   b. 25%
   c. $2
   d.* More information is needed

10. The pure union wage advantage in this market is:
   a.* 20%
   b. 25%
   c. $2
   d. More information is needed

11. The product market effect would be modeled by:
   a. shifting the nonunion supply curve to the right, increasing the measured union wage advantage
   b.* shifting the nonunion demand curve to the right, reducing the measured union wage advantage
   c. shifting the union demand curve to the right, increasing the measured union wage advantage
   d. raising the nonunion wage above its equilibrium level, reducing the true union wage advantage

12. Which one of the following contributes to the difficulty of measuring the pure union wage advantage?
   a. Women constitute a greater proportion of the work force in strongly unionized industries than in weakly unionized industries
   b.* Unionized industries tend to have larger plants that may require greater worker supervision, thus promoting union employers to seek out "superior" workers
   c. Unionized industries tend to employ production methods that are highly labor-intensive and therefore require lower-paid unskilled workers
   d. Unions are more easily established in those industries that pay low wages, so that the percentage wage gains are much smaller

13. The measured union wage advantage may *overstate* the pure union wage advantage because:
    a.* workers who lose their jobs in the union sector may seek and obtain jobs in the nonunion sector, reducing wage rates in the latter
    b. nonunion employers may increase the wages they pay their workers to reduce the likelihood their firms will become unionized
    c. workers who lose their jobs in the union sector may prefer to remain in the union sector, hoping to be recalled rather than accepting lower-paying nonunion wages
    d. unionized plants tend to be less efficient, resulting in lower marginal products of union workers

14. Hirsch and Macpherson estimate the overall union wage advantage to be approximately:
    a. 7%   b. 12%   c.* 18%   d. 24%

15. Empirical research suggests that the approximate union wage advantage in the private sector and the public sector are, respectively:
    a. 10 – 15% ; 15 – 20%   c. 15 – 20% ; 25 – 30%
    b.* 15 – 20% ; 10 – 15%   d. 25 – 30% ; 25 – 30%

16. Which one of the following is a *true* statement?
    a. The union wage advantage is smaller after fringe benefits are included
    b.* The union wage advantage is greater after fringe benefits are included
    c. Inclusion of fringe benefits has no measurable impact on the union wage advantage
    d. Because fringe benefit levels are prescribed by law, the impact of these benefits on the union wage advantage is negligible

17. The union wage advantage tends to:
    a. decrease during recessions
    b.* be larger among craft unions
    c. be smaller among blacks
    d. be smaller among lower-educated workers

18. Which one of the following is a true statement?
    a. The union wage advantage narrows during recessions
    b. There is no union wage advantage for black males
    c. Unions achieve bigger wage gains for clerical workers than workers in crafts
    d.* The union wage advantage is bigger for workers with less education than for workers with more education

19. Which one of the following does *not* explain why union workers receive more fringe benefits than nonunion workers?
    a. The unionized firm is willing to pay both higher wages and fringe benefits to avoid the costs of a strike
    b. The higher incomes of union workers allow them to "purchase" more fringe benefits
    c.* Unions are primarily composed of younger workers who have more to gain from long-term compensation such as provided by pension plans
    d. As collective voice institutions, unions may better formulate fringe benefit proposals, inform their membership of their worth, and communicate these desires to the firm

20. Unions may reduce economic efficiency by:
    a. providing an "exit" mechanism
    b. insisting promotions be based on ability rather than seniority
    c.* imposing restrictive work rules
    d. reducing worker turnover

21. Unions may increase economic efficiency by:
    a. providing an "exit" mechanism
    b. insisting promotions be based on ability rather than seniority
    c. imposing restrictive work rules
    d.* reducing worker turnover

22. Unions may increase productivity by:
    a.* providing a "voice mechanism"
    b. providing an "exit mechanism"
    c. reducing the capital/labor ratio
    d. increasing worker turnover, particularly among younger workers so that only the best employees survive

23. By reducing labor turnover, unions may increase productivity because a lower turnover rate:
    a. results in a less-experienced workforce
    b.* increases the incentive for firms to provide specific training to their workers
    c. allows firms to employ a greater number of younger, more energetic workers
    d. increases the incentive for firms to substitute labor for capital in the production process

24. Which one of the following observations supports the argument that unions *increase* productivity?
    a.* Turnover in union firms is lower than in nonunion firms
    b. Unions alter the allocation of labor between union and nonunion firms
    c. Training at union firms is lower than at nonunion firms
    d. Unions provide an "exit" option whereas nonunion workers only have a "voice" option

25. As a percentage of total work-time, the average amount of work-time lost because of strikes annually is:
    a.* less than 1%   c. 9%-10%
    b. 4%-5%   d. greater than 15%

26. Work-time lost as a result of a strike:
    a. is generally less costly in service industries than in durable-goods industries
    b. is estimated to be more costly than the efficiency losses resulting from union-caused labor misallocation
    c. may overstate the cost of a strike if struck employers are able to expand their inventories in anticipation of the strike
    d.* may understate the cost of a strike if the work stoppage disrupts production in associated industries

27. The allocative efficiency loss associated with unions arises because:
    a. job losers in the union sector take away jobs from more productive workers in the nonunion sector
    b.* the value of lost output in the union sector is greater than the value of any additional output in the nonunion sector
    c. the union wage rises above the value of marginal product while the nonunion wage falls below it
    d. job losers in the union sector are unqualified to work in the nonunion sector, so society loses their potential output

Questions 28 – 30 refer to the following graph, in which all product markets are assumed to be competitive.

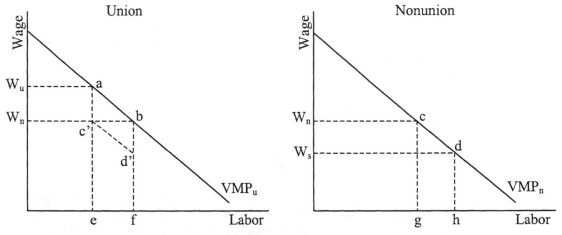

28. Assume the two labor demand curves are identical, and that all union workers who lose their job as a result of the union wage increase to W_u find jobs in the nonunion sector. The area corresponding to the efficiency loss is:
    a.* c'abd'   c. eabf
    b. $W_n W_u a$ c'   d. gcdh

29. If all displaced union workers opt to remain in the union sector hoping to be recalled, the area corresponding to the efficiency loss of the union wage increase is:
    a.* c'abd'   c.* eabf
    b. $W_n W_u a$ c'   d. gcdh

30. The allocative efficiency loss implied by the diagram is a static, short-run loss. Compared to the static loss, the dynamic, long-run loss is probably:
    a.* greater, because unions reduce firm profitability and thereby inhibit investment
    b. greater, because unemployment is greater in the long run
    c. greater, as firms have a greater opportunity to exercise their monopsony power
    d. smaller, because the decline in nonunion wages increases the extent of poverty

31. Evidence suggests that unions reduce firm profitability and discourage investment, so that:
    a. the dynamic efficiency loss from unionization is smaller than the static efficiency loss
    b.* the dynamic efficiency loss from unionization is greater than the static efficiency loss
    c. turnover in union firms is greater because workers become bored with old technology
    d. turnover in nonunion firms is greater because workers cannot keep up with new technology

32. In industry A, all displaced workers remain in the union sector waiting to be recalled. In industry B, all displaced workers seek work in the nonunion sector. All else constant, the:
    a.* allocative efficiency loss is greater in industry A
    b. allocative efficiency loss is greater in industry B
    c. allocative efficiency loss is the same in A and B
    d. dynamic efficiency loss is greater in industry A

33. Regarding unions and productivity, empirical results show that:
    a.* the impact of unionization on productivity is not clear cut
    b. unionization reduces productivity generally
    c. unionization improves productivity generally
    d. unionization improves productivity most in industries where union and management are most adversarial

34. Regarding unions and profitability, empirical results show that:
    a. unions consistently reduce profitability the most in less-concentrated industries
    b. unions consistently reduce profitability the most in more-concentrated industries
    c.* unionization reduces profitability overall
    d. unionization increases profitability overall

35. Evidence indicates that, on balance, union wage policies tend to:
    a. lead to greater overall inequality in the distribution of earnings
    b. assign wages to individual workers, whereas nonunion firms tend to assign wages to jobs
    c.* decrease the wage gap between unskilled and skilled workers by seeking equal absolute wage increases for all workers rather than equal relative wage increases
    d. raise wage rates at only the largest firms in an industry, thereby increasing wage dispersion within the industry

36. There is a general consensus among economists that:
    a. unions reduce unemployment
    b. unions increase unemployment
    c. unions have increased labor's share of national income
    d.* union wage determination is not a serious cause of inflation in the United States

37. (*World of Work* 11-1) Two-tier wage systems:
    a. have been adopted as a means of raising the relative pay of new workers who are typically females or minorities
    b.* reduce labor costs in the short run but may eventually raise them because of their adverse impacts on morale and productivity
    c. were adopted in the 1980s in response to labor shortages and the higher wage rates being commanded by new workers
    d. were adopted over the strenuous objections of current workers who demanded equal pay for equal work even if it meant significant layoffs or lower pay for everyone

38. (*World of Work* 11-2) A study by Macpherson and Stewart indicated that international competition:
    a.* has had a greater impact on union wages than nonunion wages
    b. has had a greater impact on nonunion wages than union wages
    c. has not affected the union wage advantage
    d. drove down union wages in heavily unionized industries

39.   (*World of Work* 11-3) A 1996 strike by 2700 workers at a General Motors Brake plant:
   a.   had no impact of employment of General Motors parts suppliers
   b.   had no impact on overall employment, since General Motors had stockpiled inventories of parts
   c.   lends support to the authors' conclusion that the time lost to a strike overstates the true cost of strikes
   d.*   resulted in the layoff of nearly 90,000 workers in related jobs

40.   (*World of Work* 11-4) Eberts and Stone present evidence that time spent by school principals on curriculum development and the like tended to:
   a.   have no impact on student scores
   b.   raise student test scores similarly in unionized and nonunionized schools
   c.   raise student test scores in nonunionized schools but not in unionized schools
   d.*   raise student test scores in unionized schools but not in nonunionized schools

CHAPTER 12
Government and the Labor Market: Employment, Expenditures, and Taxation

I. PUBLIC SECTOR EMPLOYMENT WAGES
    A.   Government Employment: Extent and Growth
    B.   Public- versus Private-Sector Pay

II. THE MILITARY SECTOR: THE DRAFT VERSUS THE VOLUNTARY ARMY
    A.   The Economics of Military Conscription
    B.   The Voluntary, Market-Based Approach

III. NONPAYROLL SPENDING BY GOVERNMENT: IMPACT ON LABOR
    A.   Government Purchases of Private-Sector Output
    B.   Transfer Payments and Subsidies
        1.   Demand Effects
        2.   Supply Effects

IV. LABOR MARKET EFFECTS OF PUBLICLY PROVIDED GOODS AND SERVICES
    A.   Effects on Labor Demand
    B.   Effects on Labor Supply

V. INCOME TAXATION AND THE LABOR MARKET
    A.   The Income Tax: Impact on Wages and Employment
        1.   Perfectly Inelastic Labor Supply
        2.   Positively Sloped Labor Supply
    B.   The Income Tax and Individual Labor Supply
        1.   Theoretical Analysis
            a.   Graphical Depiction
            b.   Caveat
        2.   Empirical Analysis
        3.   Specific Individuals and Markets

WORLD OF WORK
    1.   What Do Government Workers Do?
    2.   The Ten Most Unusual Federal Jobs
    3.   Public-Sector Unions: Are they Unique?
    4.   The Effect of Retention Bonuses on Reenlistment in the U.S. Army
    5.   Who Pays the Social Security Payroll Tax?

GLOBAL PERSPECTIVE
    1.   Public Sector Employment, 1995
    2.   Income Tax Rates

LEARNING OBJECTIVES

After learning the material in Chapter 12 of *Contemporary Labor Economics*, the student should be able to:

1. list the reasons for the relative growth of public sector employment over the past few decades

2. compare and contrast public-sector compensation with that in the private sector

3. distinguish the real cost of any given level of military employment from the costs as seen by taxpayers, military personnel, and Congress

4. explain why an all-volunteer military is likely to employ less labor relative to capital than a military that relies on conscription

5. show graphically and explain the short-run and long-run labor demand impacts of government provision of goods and services, both in the aggregate and in individual markets

6. describe the labor demand and supply effects of government transfers

7. show graphically how government provision of public goods creates income and substitution effects that affect labor supply

8. identify graphically the equilibrium market wage, after-tax wage, and employment level following the imposition of a tax on wage income

9. show how the incidence of wage-based taxes, all else equal, depends on the elasticity of labor supply

10. use the basic income-leisure model to graph the individual labor supply response to a tax on wage income

11. cite general empirical findings concerning the effects of various taxes on wage rates and employment

ANSWERS TO SELECTED END-OF-CHAPTER QUESTIONS

6. A reduction in governmentally provided goods reduces income with no change in the market wage. This pure income effect would reduce consumption of leisure, thereby increasing optimal work hours.

7. a. Public parks increase the demand for recreational vehicles, thereby increasing the demand for labor in that industry.
   b. If public parks are a substitute for private theme parks, the reduced demand for the private theme parks will reduce the derived demand for these workers.
   c. The pure income effect of private parks will reduce the overall supply of labor.

8. a. The tax is proportional, at a rate of 33%.
   b. Before the tax, the equilibrium wage is $6.
   c. There is no change in hours worked or the market wage; workers' take home wage is reduced by $2.
   d. If the labor supply curve were highly elastic, then hours would fall and the market wage would rise: some of the tax would be borne by the employer.

MULTIPLE CHOICE QUESTIONS

1. Which of the following best describes the growth of public-sector employment since 1950?
   a. As a percentage of total employment, state and local employment have fallen, but federal employment has risen sufficiently to cause overall public-sector employment to rise
   b. As a percentage of total employment, both federal and state and local employment have grown
   c. The absolute level of public-sector employment has grown, but has fallen as a percentage of total employment
   d.* As a percentage of total employment, federal employment has fallen, but state and local employment have risen sufficiently to cause overall public-sector employment to rise

2. Since 1950, government employment has grown:
   a. more quickly at the federal level than the state and local level
   b.* more quickly at the state and local level than the federal level
   c. as quickly at the federal level as the state and local level
   d. more quickly at the federal level than total U.S. employment has grown

3. Which of the following best explains the growth of public-sector employment relative to the private sector since 1950?
   a.* Labor supply has increased at the same pace in both sectors, but labor demand has increased more rapidly in the public sector
   b. Labor supply has increased at the same pace in both sectors, but labor demand has increased more rapidly in the private sector
   c. Labor demand has increased at the same pace in both sectors, but labor supply has increased more rapidly in the public sector
   d. Labor demand has increased at the same pace in both sectors, but labor supply has increased more rapidly in the private sector

4. A partial explanation of the change in public-sector employment since 1950 is that:
   a. the demand for public sector goods is price elastic—as their relative prices have fallen, more public goods have been demanded.
   b. the number or school-age children has declined which in turn has caused a marked decrease in the demand for public school teachers
   c.* the demand for public-sector goods is income elastic—as society's real income has grown, more public goods have been demanded
   d. the federal government has been running larger budget deficits

5. Using data from the 1970s and early 1980s, researchers have found that federal workers:
   a.* earned more than comparably educated and experienced private-sector workers
   b. earned the same as comparably educated and experienced private-sector workers
   c. earned less than comparably educated and experienced private-sector workers
   d. earned more than comparably educated and experienced private-sector workers, but this was reversed if one included fringe benefits

6. Research by Moulton and by Katz and Krueger found that:
   a. public sector wage differentials have increased in recent years
   b.* public sector wage differentials have diminished in recent years
   c. application rates for federal jobs were significantly less than for private sector jobs
   d. individual workers who moved from the private sector to the public sector experienced a wage gain of approximately 33 percent

7. In the public sector:
   a.* workers tend to receive more of their total compensation in the form of fringe benefits than their private sector counterparts
   b. workers tend to receive less of their total compensation in the form of fringe benefits than their private-sector counterparts
   c. overall wage dispersion is much greater than in the private sector
   d. quit rates are higher than in the private sector

8. Compared to their private sector counterparts, government workers:
   a. have greater labor turnover
   b.* have lower quit rates
   c. have higher and more variable rates of unemployment
   d. receive a smaller percentage of their compensation in the form of fringe benefits

9. Empirical studies of public sector pay conclude that:
   a. public-sector pay is comparable to private-sector pay, as required by law
   b. the occupational wage structure is less egalitarian than in the private sector
   c. the pay premium is greater for highly-skilled workers than for low-skilled workers
   d.* the pay premium is greater for blacks and females than for white males

Questions 10 – 12 refer to the following graph of the demand for and supply of armed forces personnel.

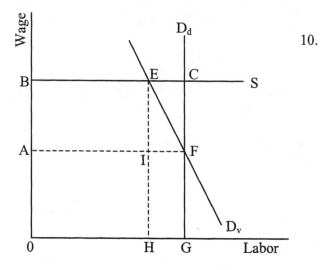

10. Suppose the government's demand for military personnel is D_d, and that it wishes to draft G persons at a wage of $A. The full cost to society of this proposal is area:
    a. 0AFG   c.* 0BCG
    b. 0BEH   d. 0BEFG

11. Suppose the government uses a voluntary system. If its demand for labor is D_v and it wishes to attract H workers at a wage of $B, which of the following best describes the distribution of costs that will result?
    a.* Taxpayers pay 0BEH; workers receive an amount equal to their opportunity costs
    b. Taxpayers pay 0BEH, workers pay ABEI
    c. Taxpayers pay 0AIH, workers pay ABEI
    d. Taxpayers pay 0BEH, workers receive ABEI

98

12. Which of the following best explains why the government demands fewer persons for the armed forces under the volunteer system than under a draft system (that is, H as compared to G)?
   a.* The higher wages of a volunteer system induce a shift to greater relative use of capital and a reduction in scale.
   b. The higher wages of a volunteer system forces the military to employ more labor relative to capital, which reduces the productivity of labor.
   c. Because a volunteer system attracts only low-wage, low-skill workers, many highly technical jobs must be eliminated.
   d. The military uses the same number of workers under either system since the true cost is independent of the system used, but it must reduce the amount of capital it uses.

13. Compared to military conscription, an all-volunteer military:
   a. is likely to substitute labor for capital
   b.* is likely to substitute capital for labor
   c. has a lower nominal cost and a lower real cost
   d. has a higher nominal cost and a higher real cost

14. Which of the following is an example of an *exhaustive* government expenditure?
   a.* Government payroll expenditures
   b. Government transfer payments
   c. Government subsidies
   d. U.S. government loans to foreign buyers of U.S. exports

15. Consider the effect on work effort of government transfers that fall as income rises (such as food stamps). Economic theory predicts that:
   a. work effort falls because the substitution effect outweighs the income effect
   b.* both the income and substitution effects tend to reduce work effort
   c. work effort rises because the substitution effect outweighs the income effect
   d. work effort falls because the income and substitution effects offset each other

16. The impact of government transfers on human capital investment decisions is best described by which of the following?
   a. In-kind transfers reduce the incentive to invest in human capital, while cash transfers increase it
   b.* Some transfers reduce the incentive to invest in human capital because higher wages are accompanied by loss of benefits; other transfers increase investment by reducing the cost of investing
   c. Transfers have a negative impact on short-run investment decisions but no impact on long-run investment decisions
   d. Transfers have no impact on human capital investment decisions

17. Suppose the federal government builds a new flood control project that takes thousands of acres of land out of agricultural production. Which of the following is most likely to occur as a result?
   a. The demand for fertilizer will rise, thereby increasing employment in that industry
   b. Wages and employment of workers who build farm equipment will rise
   c. The demand for farm workers will increase
   d.* The wages of farm workers will decline

18. Independent of taxes raised to finance it, the provision of a public good most likely:
    a.* reduces labor supply because of the income effect
    b. reduces labor supply because of the substitution effect
    c. increases labor supply if the public good is a close substitute for goods consumers otherwise would have bought
    d. has no impact on labor supply decisions

19. The provision of a public good that is complementary to leisure will:
    a. necessarily decrease labor demand in the private sector
    b. necessarily increase labor demand in the private sector
    c. likely reduce wage rates of government workers
    d.* likely reduce work effort

20. The provision of a public good that is a substitute for a private good will:
    a.* likely decrease labor demand in the private sector
    b. likely increase labor demand in the private sector
    c. necessarily reduce wage rates of government workers
    d. necessarily reduce work effort

Questions 21 and 22 refer to the following diagram.

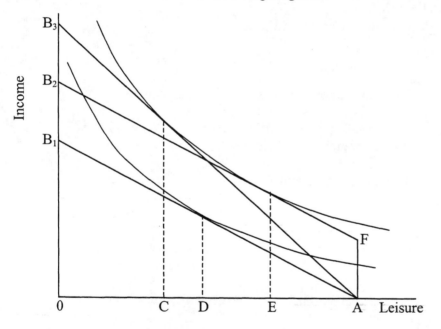

21. The worker's current budget line is given by line AB_1. The provision of a public good is best modeled by the shift to budget line:
    a. AB_3 and the subsequent increase in work hours to AC
    b. AB_3 and the subsequent decrease in work hours to AE
    c. AFB_2 and the subsequent increase in work hours to AC
    d.* AFB_2 and the subsequent decrease in work hours to AE

22. As illustrated, this public good is likely:
    a.* complementary with leisure   c. financed by a tax on payroll
    b. complementary with work   d. financed by a tax on income

100

Question 23 and 24 refer to the following diagram.

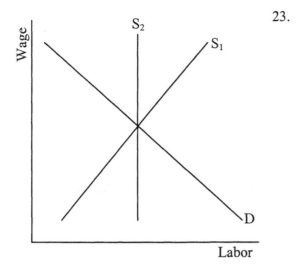

23. Assuming that labor supply is S_1, imposing an income tax on this market will:
   a.* raise the market wage rate but reduce the net (after-tax) wage rate
   b. reduce the market rate and reduce the net (after-tax) wage rate
   c. raise the market wage rate but have no impact on the net (after-tax) wage rate
   d. have no impact on the market wage rate but reduce the net (after-tax) wage rate

24. Assuming that labor supply is S_2, imposing an income tax on this market will:
   a. raise the market wage rate but reduce the net (after-tax) wage rate
   b. reduce the market wage rate and reduce the net (after-tax) wage rate
   c. raise the market wage rate but have no impact on the net (after-tax) wage rate
   d.* have no impact on the market wage rate but reduce the net (after-tax) wage rate

25. To pay for new health care reforms, suppose a new payroll tax is levied on employers. The economic burden of the new tax will fall:
   a. on employers because the payroll tax is collected from them
   b. more on workers the more elastic is the labor supply curve
   c.* more on workers the more inelastic is the labor supply curve
   d. entirely on workers as long as the labor supply curve slopes upward

26. Suppose the aggregate labor supply curve slopes upward and the income tax rate is increased. Economic theory predicts that the employment of labor will _____ and the after-tax "take-home" wage will _____.
   a. not change, fall   c.* fall, fall
   b. not change, not change   d. fall, not change

27. For any given individual, an increase in the income tax rate will:
   a. increase work effort
   b. decrease work effort
   c. decrease work effort if the income effect outweighs the substitution effect
   d.* increase work effort if the income effect outweighs the substitution effect

28. According to the theory of *individual* labor supply, a reduction in income tax rates leads to:
   a. a reduction in hours worked
   b. an increase in hours worked
   c. no change in hours worked
   d.* an unpredictable change in hours worked

29.   Most studies conclude that aggregate labor supply is very:
       a.   elastic, so that income taxes are borne mainly by workers
       b.*   inelastic, so that income taxes are borne mainly by workers
       c.   elastic, so that income taxes are borne mainly by employers
       d.   inelastic, so that income taxes are borne mainly by employers

30.   Suppose the payroll tax is increased. For any given labor demand, the greater the elasticity of
       supply:
       a.   the greater the decline in both the net (after-tax) wage rate and employment
       b.   the less the decline in both the net (after-tax) wage rate and employment
       c.   the greater the decline in the net (after-tax) wage rate and the less the decline in
              employment
       d.*   the less the decline in the net (after-tax) wage rate and the greater the decline in
              employment

31.   If labor supply is perfectly inelastic, the economic incidence of the payroll tax:
       a.   is the same as the statutory incidence of the tax
       b.   is split equally between workers and consumers, because firms pass on their share in the
              form of higher prices
       c.   falls entirely on firms
       d.*   falls entirely on workers

32.   According to empirical evidence, most of the burden of the payroll tax appears to fall on workers,
       even though about half is supposedly "paid" by their employers. This observation is attributed to
       the finding that:
       a.   many workers are self-employed and must pay the full amount of a payroll tax
       b.*   the aggregate supply of labor tends to be relatively inelastic
       c.   the aggregate demand for labor tends to be relatively inelastic
       d.   employers have much stronger bargaining power than workers since only a tiny fraction
              of the labor force is unionized

33.   (*World of Work* 12-1) Which function currently accounts for the greatest percentage of state and
       local workers?
       a.   General administration   c.   Public welfare
       b.   Police and fire protection   d.*   Education

34.   (*World of Work* 12-3) According to Freeman, public sector unions:
       a.   have extraordinary bargaining power because of the government's monopoly provision of
              services
       b.*   are unique because of the political nature of public sector collective bargaining
       c.   have no bargaining power at all because they cannot strike legally
       d.   have great bargaining power because governments face binding tax and budget
              constraints

35.   (*World of Work* 12-4) In the armed forces, retention bonuses appear to increase reenlistment rates.
       The effect is stronger for _____ personnel, probably because their training is _____.
       a.   non-combat; specific   c.*   combat; specific
       b.   non-combat; general   d.   combat, general

36.   (*World of Work* 12-5) According to research on the incidence of Social Security payroll taxes:

a.   workers and firms bear the social security tax equally

b.   workers bear a greater share of the social security tax burden than firms, because firms "collect" some of the taxes for customers in the form of higher output prices

c.*   workers bear a greater share of the social security tax burden than firms, because firms "collect" some of the taxes from workers in the form of reduced wages

d.   firms bear a greater share of the social security tax burden than workers, because workers "collect" some of the tax proceeds from firms in the form of increased wages

CHAPTER 13
Government and the Labor Market: Legislation and Regulation

I.   LABOR LAW
    A.   Labor Law and Union Membership
        1.   Labor Law and Private-Sector Union Membership
            a.   Pre-1930 period
            b.   Post-1930 period
        2.   Labor Law and Public-Sector Union Membership
    B.   Labor Law and Bargaining Power
        1.   Limitation on the Use of the Injunction
        2.   Prohibition of Secondary Boycotts

II.   MINIMUM-WAGE LAW
    A.   Facts and Controversy
    B.   The Competitive Model
        1.   Complete Coverage
        2.   Incomplete Coverage
    C.   The Shock Effect
    D.   Monopsony
    E.   Other Considerations
        1.   Union Support
        2.   Efficiency Wage Considerations
    F.   Empirical Evidence
        1.   Employment and Unemployment
            a.   Teenagers
            b.   Young Adults
            c.   Older Adults
        2.   Investment in Human Capital
        3.   Income Inequality and Poverty
    G.   Final Remarks

III. OCCUPATIONAL HEALTH AND SAFETY REGULATION
    A.   Profit-Maximizing Level of Job Safety
    B.   Society's Optimal Level of Job Safety
        1.   Perfect Information and Assessment
        2.   Imperfect Information and Assessment
    C.   The Occupational Safety and Health Act
        1.   The Case for OSHA
        2.   Criticisms of OSHA
        3.   Findings and Implications

IV.   GOVERNMENT AS A RENT PROVIDER
    A.   Occupational Licensure
    B.   Tariffs, Quotas, and Domestic Content Rules

WORLD OF WORK
1. Surprising New Findings on the Minimum Wage
2. Do Computers Expand Job Opportunities for Those with Spinal Cord Injuries?
3. The Effect of Workers' Compensation on Job Safety
4. Turf Wars

GLOBAL PERSPECTIVE
1. Occupational Injuries, 1991 – 1993

LEARNING OBJECTIVES

After learning the material in Chapter 13 of *Contemporary Labor Economics*, the student should be able to:

1. identify the major pieces of U.S. labor relations legislation and state the impact each has had on the growth of unions and union membership

2. explain the effects of the major labor laws on union bargaining power, especially with respect to labor market wage and employment levels

3. use both a one-sector and a two-sector model to show graphically and analyze the likely labor market impacts of the minimum wage

4. list those factors that suggest that the disemployment effects of the minimum wage might be less than is predicted by the competitive model

5. identify the limits within which a minimum wage will increase the employment of a firm possessing monopsony power

6. describe the findings of empirical research concerning the overall impacts of the minimum wage with respect to the size and composition of the labor force, employment, investment in human capital, allocative efficiency, income inequality, and the reduction of poverty

7. describe the incentives of a profit-maximizing firm to provide job safety and determine whether such a firm will provide the socially optimal level of safety

8. analyze the arguments for and against workplace safety standards as embodied in the Occupational Safety and Health Act of 1970

9. evaluate the results of research on the impact of OSHA on workplace safety

10. graphically determine the changes in economic rent that arise from occupation licensure, tariffs and quotas, local content rules and other examples of government rule-making

ANSWERS TO SELECTED END-OF-CHAPTER QUESTIONS

2. Each of the changes would increase union bargaining power by increasing management's cost of disagreeing.

5. a. If some of the teenagers who cannot find jobs drop out of the labor force, teen employment could fall without a rise in the teen unemployment rate.
   b. General training may fall because it is difficult to reduce the starting wage during the training period. Formal schooling may increase because with fewer job opportunities the perceived benefit of quitting school may fall.

c.   The resulting increase in unemployment (reduced probability of finding a job) may increase the perceived cost of shirking, reducing the wage premium required to prevent such behavior.

6.   Higher minimum wages can drive up the cost of employing low-skilled labor. This will increase the demand for union labor if low-skilled labor and union labor are gross substitutes.

In the latter case, union labor is a complement in production with materials produced by low-skilled labor. The increase in the minimum wage will drive up the price of these materials and thereby decrease the demand for union labor.

8.   a.   4 units: the marginal benefit of the fifth unit is less than its marginal cost.
     b.   4 units: the firm's marginal benefits and marginal costs reflect the social benefits and costs.
     c.   The marginal cost ($15) exceeds the marginal benefit ($6). Workers may object because the safer work environment will increase labor supply, reducing the compensating wage differential.
     d.   It would now be profitable to provide the fifth unit of safety.

MULTIPLE CHOICE QUESTIONS

1.   Prior to the 1930s, union membership growth was relatively:
     a.*   slow, due to the use of blacklisting, injunctions, and yellow dog contracts
     b.   slow, due to the widespread use of lockouts and strikebreakers authorized under the Norris-LaGuardia act
     c.   rapid, due to the favorable court treatment of union activity provided by passage of the Sherman Act of 1890
     d.   rapid, due to favorable court interpretations concerning workers' property rights

2.   "Yellow-dog contracts":
     a.*   were used by employers to restrict union membership
     b.   require workers to join a union as a condition of continued employment
     c.   were upheld by the Taft-Hartley Act
     d.   were outlawed by the Landrum-Griffin Act

3.   The "twin rights" of labor (self-organization and collective bargaining) were guaranteed by the:
     a.   Fair Labor Standards Act   c.   Taft-Hartley Act
     b.*   Wagner Act   d.   Landrum-Griffin Act

4.   Which one of the following would be viewed by organized labor as a contributor to union membership?
     a.   Landrum-Griffin Act   c.   Sherman Act
     b.*   Norris-LaGuardia Act   d.   Taft-Hartley Act

5.   Which of the following outlawed company unions?
     a.   Fair Labor Standards Act   c.   Taft-Hartley Act
     b.*   Wagner Act   d.   Landrum-Griffin Act

6. Which of the following gave states the option to pass so-called "right-to-work" laws?
   - a. Fair Labor Standards Act
   - c.* Taft-Hartley Act
   - b. Wagner Act
   - d. Landrum-Griffin Act

7. Public sector union growth was most encouraged by:
   - a. the Wagner Act
   - b. the Taft-Hartley Act
   - c. The Landrum-Griffin Act
   - d.* a series of executive orders and state laws recognizing the rights of public sector workers to organize

8. Which one of the following laws most dramatically increased union bargaining power?
   - a. Sherman Act
   - c. Taft-Hartley Act
   - b.* Wagner Act
   - d. Landrum-Griffin Act

9. The prohibition of secondary boycotts:
   - a. reduced management's bargaining power by reducing the union's cost of disagreeing
   - b. reduced management's bargaining power by reducing management's cost of disagreeing
   - c.* increased management's bargaining power by increasing the union's cost of disagreeing
   - d. increased management's bargaining power by increasing management's cost of disagreeing

10. Which one of the following established unfair labor practices by employers?
    - a. Norris-LaGuardia Act
    - c.* Wagner Act
    - b. Taft-Hartley Act
    - d. Landrum-Griffin Act

11. Which one of the following established unfair labor practices by unions?
    - a. Norris-LaGuardia Act
    - c. Wagner Act
    - b.* Taft-Hartley Act
    - d. Landrum-Griffin Act

12. According to the Wagner Act, which of the following is *not* an unfair labor practice by employers?
    - a. Firing an employee who joins or sympathizes with a union
    - b. Establishing a company union
    - c. Interfering with union organizing activity
    - d.* Failing to reach a collective bargaining agreement after bargaining in good faith

13. According to the Taft-Hartley Act, which of the following is *not* an unfair labor practice by unions?
    - a. Striking a company over a jurisdictional dispute with another union
    - b.* Striking a company as a means of trying to obtain a collective bargaining agreement with that firm
    - c. Striking a company to show sympathy for another union in obtaining employer recognition
    - d. Setting excessive union dues

14. Which one of the following required unions to hold regularly scheduled elections of union officers?
    - a. Norris-LaGuardia Act
    - c. Wagner Act
    - b. Taft-Hartley Act
    - d.* Landrum-Griffin Act

15. A majority of the workers earning the minimum wage:
     a.   are males   c.   work full-time
     b.* are females   d.   are teenagers

16. Currently, the minimum wage law does not apply to about 12% of non-supervisory workers.
     Assuming that all consequently displaced workers find jobs in the uncovered sector, an increase
     in the minimum wage will:
     a.   make all workers better off
     b.   cause a migration of workers from the uncovered to the covered sector
     c.* create additional output in the uncovered sector of a lower value than the output lost in
          the covered sector
     d.   cause an increase in economic rent to original workers in the uncovered sector

17. Which one of the following claims concerning the minimum wage is generally supported by
     empirical evidence?
     a.* The minimum wage has only a minor impact on the overall degree of income inequality
     b.   The minimum wage has increased teenage employment as a result of the shock effect
     c.   Union members suffer the greatest negative impacts of the minimum wage
     d.   The reduction in teen employment due to the minimum wage is less than the increase in
          unemployment

Answer questions 18 – 20 on the basis of the following diagram:

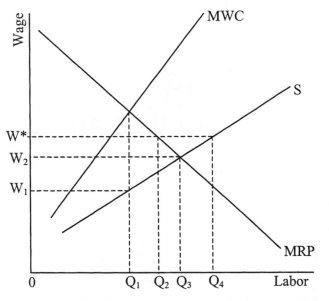

18. Suppose this labor market is
     competitive, so that the wage rate is
     W_2. If W^* is imposed as the minimum
     wage, then employment in this market:
     a.   will rise
     b.* will fall
     c.   will remain the same
     d.   may or may not change; more
          information is required

19. Suppose this labor market is competitive, so that the wage rate is W_2. W^* is then imposed as the
     minimum wage. If the minimum wage shocks management into more efficient resource use:
     a.* the demand curve will shift to the right and employment will not fall as far as Q_2
     b.   the supply curve will shift to the right and employment will expand beyond Q_2
     c.   employment will not fall from its competitive level
     d.   the supply curve will shift to the left until it intersects demand at W^*

20. Suppose this labor market is monopsonistic, so that the wage is W_1. If W^* is imposed as the
     minimum wage, then employment in this market:
     a.* will rise to Q_2 c.   will fall
     b.   will rise to Q_4 d.   will remain the same

21. A monopsonist is currently paying its 1,000 workers $5.00 per hour. Its marginal wage cost is $6.00 per hour, however. If the government sets a minimum wage of $5.50, then:
a.* employment at this firm will rise
b. employment at this firm will fall
c. employment at this firm will be unaffected
d. employment at this firm will rise but the firm's total wage bill will fall

22. Increases in the minimum wage tend to:
a. increase both formal schooling and general on-the-job training
b. increase formal schooling and reduce general on-the-job training
c. reduce formal schooling and increase general on-the-job training
d.* reduce both formal schooling and general on-the-job training

23. Unions will generally support an increase in the minimum wage:
a. if union workers are gross complements with minimum wage workers
b.* if union workers are gross substitutes with minimum wage workers
c. if union workers represent a large percentage of total labor costs
d. if union workers represent a small percentage of total labor costs

24. If some firms pay efficiency wages, an increase in the minimum wage may:
a. increase total unemployment by increasing the efficiency wage
b. increase total unemployment by reducing the efficiency wage
c. reduce total unemployment by increasing the efficiency wage
d.* reduce total unemployment by reducing the efficiency wage

25. Unemployment impacts of any increase in the minimum wage tend to be greatest for:
a.* teens   c. prime-age workers
b. young adults   d. older adults

26. Which of the following is given as a justification of the health and safety standards established by OSHA?
a. Workers overestimate the amount of risk associated with jobs, resulting in a larger than optimal wage premium for hazardous jobs
b. Workers underestimate the amount of risk associated with jobs, resulting in a larger than optimal wage premium for hazardous jobs
c. Firm overestimate the amount of risk associated with jobs, resulting in a smaller than optimal wage premium for hazardous jobs
d.* Information and occupational mobility are imperfect, so that the wage premium for job safety provides inadequate incentive for firms to provide safety

27. Firms will cut back on job safety as long as:
a.* potential cost savings are at least as great as wage increases that might have to be paid to attract labor
b. potential cost savings are less than wage increases that might have to be paid to attract labor
c. the marginal cost of safety is positive
d. the marginal benefit of safety to the firm is very large

Answer questions 28 and 29 on the basis of the following table, in which MB_s and MC_s are the marginal benefit and marginal cost of safety, respectively. P_s is the probability that a worker will not suffer an injury on the job during a one year period, and is thus a measure of job safety.

P_s	MB_s	MC_s
.65	25	8
.70	22	10
.75	19	12
.80	16	14
.85	13	16
.90	10	18
.95	7	20

28. The profit-maximizing level of job safety is a probability level of:
    a.   0.65   c.*   0.80
    b.   0.75   d.   0.85

29. If workers underestimate the actual amount of risk associated with the job because of imperfect information, the values in the:
    a.* MB_s column will understate the true marginal benefit and the profit-maximizing level of job safety will be less than the optimal level
    b. MB_s column will overstate the true marginal benefit and profit-maximizing level of job safety will exceed the optimal level
    c. MC_s column will overstate the true marginal cost and the profit-maximizing level of job safety will exceed the optimal level
    d. MC_s column will understate the true marginal cost and the profit-maximizing level of job safety will exceed the optimal level

30. Which of the following best describes the amount of job safety?
    a.   Firms have no incentive to provide a safe environment, so there is too little safety
    b.   Only unionized firms can negotiate for a safe environment, so they have safe jobs while nonunion workers must work in unsafe environments
    c.   Firms have some incentive to provide safety, but imperfect information and labor immobility lead safety to be over-provided
    d.*   Firms have some incentive to provide safety, but imperfect information and labor immobility lead safety to be under-provided

31. Empirical estimates of OSHA's effectiveness at reducing risk of injury and death on the job have:
    a.*   been mixed
    b.   shown no changes at all in fatal or non-fatal injuries
    c.   shown reductions in both fatal and non-fatal injury rates
    d.   shown increases in both fatal and nonfatal injury rates

32. Consider a proposed law to deregulate the hair-care industry. Barbers would be allowed to do work previously confined to stylists, and the latter would no longer be required to pass strict licensure exams. Which outcome would you expect to result from this deregulation?
    a.*   A decrease in economic rent to current stylists
    b.   A decrease in economic rent to current barbers
    c.   An increase in economic rent to beauty school operators
    d.   An increase in economic rent to workers in occupations in which displaced stylists find jobs

33.　Suppose a state law is passed which prohibits the state liquor board from issuing any new liquor licenses. (Such licenses are required to sell liquor.) The law would allow prospective tavern operators to purchase an existing license on the open market from a willing current owner of such a license. Which outcome would you expect to result from this regulation?
　　a.　　A decrease in economic rent to current holders of liquor licenses
　　b.*　An increase in economic rent to current holders of liquor licenses
　　c.　　An increase in economic rent to prospective operators of taverns
　　d.　　No change in economic rent to prospective operators of taverns

Answer questions 34 and 35 on the basis of the following diagram:

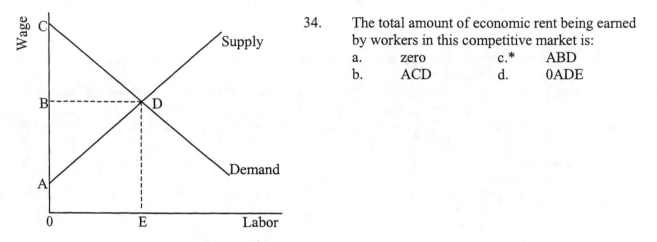

34.　The total amount of economic rent being earned by workers in this competitive market is:
　　a.　　zero　　　　　c.*　ABD
　　b.　　ACD　　　　　d.　0ADE

35.　Suppose this represents the market for U.S. autoworkers. If the government were to pass legislation mandating that all vehicles sold in the U.S. contain at least 50% domestically produced or assembled components, then:
　　a.　　supply would shift to the right, reducing economic rent to U.S. autoworkers
　　b.　　supply would shift to the left, reducing economic rent to U.S. autoworkers
　　c.　　demand would shift to the right, reducing economic rent to U.S. autoworkers
　　d.*　demand would shift to the right, increasing economic rent to U.S. autoworkers

36.　A "domestic content" law for automobiles would increase the economic rent of workers in the U.S. automobile industry by:
　　a.　　decreasing the demand for autoworkers in the U.S.
　　b.　　decreasing the supply of U.S. autoworkers in the U.S.
　　c.　　allowing U.S. autoworkers to obtain higher wages even though employment falls in the U.S. automobile industry
　　d.*　increasing the demand for autoworkers in the U.S. and pushing up their wages

37.　Which of the following would unambiguously increase the economic rent of *current* dental assistants?
　　a.*　Requiring all future dental assistants to get an advanced degree
　　b.　　Requiring all current and future dental assistants to get an advanced degree
　　c.　　Requiring all current dental assistants to get an advanced degree
　　d.　　Requiring all dental assistants to work under the direct supervision of a dentist

Question 38 refers to the following diagram:

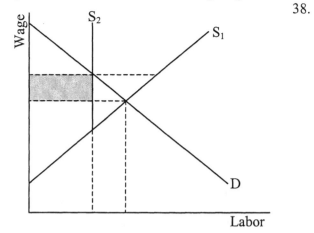

38. The increase in economic rent shown in the diagram is consistent with:
   a.* setting a limit on the number of licensed employees in this occupation
   b. imposing a tariff on similar products produced by foreigners
   c. imposing a quota on similar products produced by foreigners
   d. imposing a requirement that all future employees in this occupation obtain an advanced degree

39. (*World of Work* 13-1) Examining evidence on the impacts of increases in state minimum wages in New Jersey and California, Card and Krueger found:
   a. substantial reductions in employment, particularly among teens
   b. no increases in wages of low-wage workers, because employers flouted the law
   c.* no evidence of reductions in employment
   d. poor quality of the data collected by Neumark and Wascher

40. (*World of Work* 13-2) In their analysis of New Jersey residents with spinal cord injuries, Krueger, Kruse, and Drastal concluded that:
   a. these workers have the same employment rates as the general population
   b. these workers suffer substantial drops in wage rates for those who remain working
   c. computer use had no impact on wage rates or employment of disabled workers
   d.* computer skills are associated with increased wages and faster earnings growth for disabled workers

41. (*World of Work* 13-3) With respect to workers' compensation insurance, research by Moore and Viscusi indicates that job fatalities are:
   a.* reduced because the positive incentive effect swamps the negative moral hazard effect of the law
   b. reduced because the negative moral hazard effect swamps the positive incentive effect of the law
   c. increased because the positive incentive effect swamps the negative moral hazard effect of the law
   d. increased because the negative moral hazard effect swarms the positive incentive effect of the law

42. (*World of Work* 13-4) "Turf wars" occur when:
   a. economic rents are not available
   b. occupational licensure does not occur
   c.* occupational groups seek licensure, which is opposed by other occupations
   d. there are minimum wage laws

CHAPTER 14
Labor Market Discrimination

I. DISCRIMINATION AND ITS DIMENSIONS
- A. Types of Discrimination
  - 1. Wage Discrimination
  - 2. Employment Discrimination
  - 3. Occupational or Job Discrimination
  - 4. Human Capital Discrimination
- B. Theories of Labor Market Discrimination

II. TASTE-FOR-DISCRIMINATION MODEL
- A. The Discrimination Coefficient
- B. Demand and Supply Interpretation
- C. Two Generalizations
- D. Gainers, Losers, and the Persistence of Discrimination

III. MARKET POWER: THE MONOPSONY MODEL
- A. The Model
- B. Implications
- C. Elasticity Assumptions
- D. Assessment

IV. THEORY OF STATISTICAL DISCRIMINATION

V. THE CROWDING MODEL: OCCUPATIONAL SEGREGATION
- A. Assumptions and Predictions
- B. Ending Discrimination
- C. Index of Segregation
- D. Evidence

WORLD OF WORK
- 1. Sexual Harassment Global Problem
- 2. It Pays to be Good Looking
- 3. John S. Mill and Harriet Taylor Mill on Occupational Segregation
- 4. Women's Entry into Selected Professions

GLOBAL PERSPECTIVE
- 1. Occupational Segregation

LEARNING OBJECTIVES

After learning the material in Chapter 14 of *Contemporary Labor Economics*, the student should be able to:

1. distinguish between wage, employment, occupational, and human capital discrimination

2. derive equilibrium values of discrimination-based wage differentials using a modified demand and supply version of Becker's taste-for-discrimination model

3. summarize and evaluate the taste-for-discrimination model

4. describe how labor markets eliminate some forms of discrimination and perpetuate other forms

5. for a discriminating monopolist, graphically determine the wage rate and employment across demographic groups and explain how these equilibrium values are related to supply elasticities

6. summarize and evaluate the monopsony model of discrimination

7. identify conditions under which statistical discrimination may be observed

8. summarize and evaluate the statistical discrimination model

9. graphically illustrate the effects and economic costs of occupational segregation

10. summarize and evaluate the crowding model of occupational segregation

11. compute an index of segregation and indicate how this index has changed over the past 30 years

ANSWERS TO SELECTED END-OF-CHAPTER QUESTIONS

2. *d* is the amount by which a discriminating employer perceives a person's wage to exceed his or her actual wage. At the given values, equally productive whites are perceived to be cheaper; the employer will hire only whites. A decrease in the supply of black labor would increase the black-white wage ratio. An increase in employer prejudice would reduce the black-white wage ratio.

3. The conclusion rests on the assumption that female labor supply is less elastic.

5. Crowding effectively reduces labor supply in predominantly male occupations, raising wages for males, while increasing labor supply in predominantly female occupations, lowering wages for females. The elimination of crowding would raise wage rates for females and lower wage rates for males. The reallocation of labor would provide a net gain to society by equalizing VMPs.

7. In the example, the index of segregation is 70%, or 0.70. An index of 100% implies complete segregation; an index of 0% implies the sexes are represented in each occupation according to their proportion in the labor force. In the United States, the index of occupational segregation by gender declined modestly between 1973 and 1994, from 68.5% to 54.6%.

MULTIPLE CHOICE QUESTIONS

1. Discrimination in the form of access barriers to productivity-increasing opportunities is termed:
   a. wage discrimination
   b. employment discrimination
   c. occupational discrimination
   d.* human capital discrimination

2. Discrimination that results in the payment of a lower wage rate to a female relative to an equally productive male is called:
    a.*   wage discrimination   c.   occupational discrimination
    b.   employment discrimination   d.   human capital discrimination

3. If a black woman is paid a lower wage than a similarly qualified and experienced man performing the same job at the same firm, then this is an example of:
    a.*   wage discrimination   c.   occupational discrimination
    b.   employment discrimination   d.   human capital discrimination

4. Discrimination that segregates qualified women into lower paying jobs is called:
    a.   wage discrimination   c.*   occupational discrimination
    b.   employment discrimination   d.   human capital discrimination

5. An employer who is willing to pay a wage premium to avoid employing persons from some particular group is engaging in:
    a.*   a taste for discrimination   c.   statistical discrimination
    b.   monopsonistic discrimination   d.   human capital discrimination

6. Which of the following exemplifies occupational discrimination?
    a.*   97% of all secretaries are women
    b.   women secretaries make, on average, 40% of their boss' pay while male secretaries average 50% of their boss' pay
    c.   women secretaries average 12 years of education and obtain little on-the-job training; male secretaries average 12.5 years of education and usually qualify for advanced training programs
    d.   the unemployment rate for women secretaries is typically 2% higher than that for male secretaries

7. Which one of the following is an example of *premarket* discrimination:
    a.   wage discrimination   c.   occupational discrimination
    b.   employment discrimination   d.*   human capital discrimination

8. If men in occupation X earn $20 per hour and women in occupation Y earn $20 per hour, then:
    a.   there is no discrimination
    b.   there is discrimination against women if their marginal revenue product in occupation Y is lower than the marginal revenue product of men in occupation X
    c.*   there is discrimination against women if their marginal revenue product in occupation Y is higher than the marginal revenue product of men in occupation X
    d.   there is statistical discrimination against women

9. Assume that all workers are equally productive, but that male wages are $14 and female wages are $10. An employer who employs only male workers has a discrimination coefficient of:
    a.   at most 0.4   c.   at most $4
    b.*   at least $4   d.   at least 10/14

10. An employer whose discrimination coefficient is zero:
    a.   refuses to hire any women or minorities regardless of the wage rate
    b.*   does not discriminate against women or minorities
    c.   discriminates against women and minorities
    d.   discriminates in favor of women and minorities

11. An employer whose discrimination coefficient approaches infinity:
    a.* refuses to hire any women or minorities regardless of the wage rate
    b. does not discriminate against women or minorities
    c. discriminates against women but not minorities
    d. discriminates in favor of women and minorities

12. According to Becker's "taste-for-discrimination" model:
    a. firms that discriminate will have lower costs than non-discriminating firms
    b.* the existence of competitive market forces will cause discrimination to diminish and eventually disappear
    c. an increase in the supply of black workers will cause the equilibrium black/white wage ratio to rise
    d. non-discriminating firms will be put at a competitive disadvantage because they employ victims of discrimination

13. According to Becker's "taste-for-discrimination" model:
    a. a person is judged on the basis of the average characteristics of her or his demographic group
    b. the process of competition will cause discrimination-based wage differentials to persist over long periods of time
    c. there will be discrimination-based wage differentials because a firm with market power distinguishes between different groups with different elasticities of labor supply
    d.* the process of competition should put discriminating employers at a competitive disadvantage

Questions 14 and 15 refer to the following diagram, in which W_b/W_w is the ratio of the black wage rate to the white wage rate:

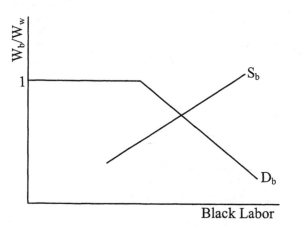

Black Labor

14. The demand curve in the diagram eventually slopes downward because:
    a.* as the black/white wage ratio falls, more firms find it "too costly" to indulge their tastes for discrimination
    b. as the black/white wage ratio rises, more firms find it "too costly" to indulge their tastes for discrimination
    c. as the black/white wage ratio falls, firms find it "less costly" to indulge their tastes for discrimination
    d. as the black/white wage ratio falls, firms will reduce their discrimination coefficients

15. The horizontal portion of the demand curve will be extended by an increase in the:
    a. number of firms that discriminate
    b.* number of firms that do not discriminate
    c. productivity of white workers
    d. supply of black workers

16. According to the "demand and supply" interpretation of Becker's model, which one of the following will tend to reduce the male-female wage gap?
    a.   An increase in the supply of female labor
    b.   An increase in the discrimination coefficients of some employers
    c.*   An increase in the number of nondiscriminating firms
    d.   An overall increase in the demand for labor

17. According to the market power (monopsony) model of discrimination:
    a.   the marginal wage cost of hiring females will exceed that of males
    b.*   wage rates for blacks will be lower than for whites if black labor supply curves are less elastic than white labor supply curves
    c.   firms that discriminate will have lower profits than if they do not discriminate
    d.   female wage rates will be lower than male wage rates if female labor demand curves are more elastic than male labor demand curves.

Answer questions 18 and 19 on the basis of the following diagram that shows the total labor supply curve and corresponding marginal wage cost curve as well as the labor supply curves and corresponding marginal wage cost curves for females and males.

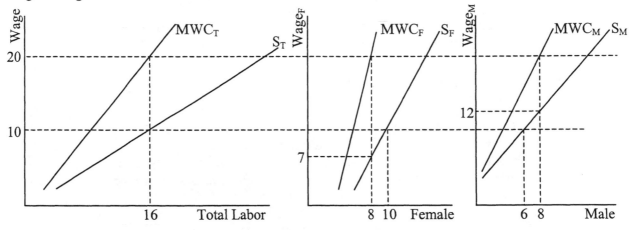

18. If this monopsonist *does not* discriminate, profits will be maximized by hiring:
    a.   8 women at a wage rate of $7 and 8 men at a wage rate of $12
    b.   8 women and 8 men, each at a wage rate of $10
    c.*   10 women and 6 men, each at a wage rate of $10
    d.   8 women at a wage rate of $7 and 6 men at a wage rate of $10

19. If this monopsonist discriminates, profits will be maximized by hiring:
    a.*   8 women at a wage rate of $7 and 8 men at a wage rate of $12
    b.   8 women and 8 men, each at a wage rate of $10
    c.   10 women and 6 men, each at a wage rate of $10
    d.   8 women at a wage rate of $7 and 6 men at a wage rate of $10

20. According to the monopsony model of discrimination:
    a.   the process of competition puts discriminating employers at a competitive disadvantage
    b.   the discrimination coefficient is a measure of prejudice in the labor market
    c.*   wage differentials may arise because a firm with market power distinguishes between different groups with different elasticities of labor supply
    d.   a person is judged on the basis of the average characteristics of her/his demographic group

21. In the monopsony model of discrimination:
   a. firms cannot sustain profits from their discriminatory behavior
   b. discrimination is malicious, because the employer seeks to avoid employing persons from a particular group
   c. market forces will cause discrimination to diminish over time
   d.* discrimination need not be rooted in malicious behavior on the part of the employer

22. Which one of the following is a criticism of the market power model of discrimination?
   a. The model relies on employer prejudice
   b. Wage discrimination is not profitable for the employer
   c.* Evidence suggests that the supply responses of women to wage changes may be greater than those of men
   d. It fails to explain the persistence of wage discrimination

23. Statistical discrimination is:
   a.* the use of some observable characteristic by employers as a screening device in the hiring process
   b. comparing the marginal productivities of job applicants to determine who is most suitable for the job
   c. not based on accumulated factual evidence about different groups
   d. malicious treatment aimed at persons with observable demographic characteristics

24. According to the theory of statistical discrimination:
   a. the process of competition should put discriminating employers at a competitive disadvantage
   b. the discrimination coefficient is a measure of prejudice in the labor market
   c. there will be discriminatory wage differentials because a firm with market power distinguishes between different groups with different elasticities of labor supply
   d.* a person is judged on the basis of the average characteristics of her or his demographic group

25. Assuming competitive labor markets, occupational segregation by sex:
   a. increases the profits of firms that discriminate
   b. is beneficial from society's standpoint, because the gains to male employees outweigh the losses to female employees
   c.* results in an inefficient allocation of labor and diminished output
   d. cannot persist, as employers will find it in their best interest to hire only female employees

26. Occupational segregation creates:
   a. a redistribution of a larger national output
   b.* a redistribution of a smaller national output
   b. a larger national output but no redistribution
   c. a smaller national output but no redistribution

27. An implication of the crowding model of segregation is that:
   a. labor must be efficiently allocated since all workers are employed
   b. the value of national output is unaffected by the segregation
   c. men's and women's wages would both rise if segregation were reduced
   d.* the value of national output is reduced by the segregation

Question 28 refers to the following labor market data showing the distribution of males and females within the three occupations (labeled A, B, and C) of a hypothetical economy.

Occupation	Male	Female
A	30%	10%
B	40%	20%
C	30%	70%

28. The index of segregation for this economy is:
    a. .20
    b. .30
    c.* .40
    d. .70

29. The index of occupational segregation by sex:
    a.* fell between 1973 and 1994
    b. increased between 1958 and 1973
    c. increased between 1973 and 1994
    d. increased between 1973 and 1994 for whites only

30. (*World of Work* 14-1) According to a report by the International Labor Organization:
    a. most nations surveyed have laws defining sexual harassment
    b.* most nations surveyed do not have laws defining sexual harassment
    c. most nations surveyed did not report incidents of sexual harassment
    d. sexual harassment appears to be confined to the United States

31. (*World of Work* 14-2) In their study of beauty and earnings, Hamermesh and Biddle report that:
    a.* attractive people enter into occupations where appearance is productive, but also earn more than plain people in jobs where beauty does not affect productivity
    b. attractive people enter into occupations where appearance is productive, but earn no more than plain people in jobs where beauty does not affect productivity
    c. less attractive people compensate for lower individual earnings by marrying persons with higher than average earnings
    d. beauty appears to have no impact on a person's earnings

32. (*World of Work* 14-3) The argument that occupational segregation is economically inefficient:
    a. was supported by Harriet Taylor Mill but refuted by John Stuart Mill
    b. was refuted by both Harriet Taylor Mill and John Stuart Mill
    c. is comparatively recent, a twentieth century phenomenon that coincides with increased female labor force participation
    d.* can be traced back at least as far as the nineteenth century, to writers like John Stuart Mill and Harriet Taylor Mill

33. (*World of Work* 14-4) The overall index of occupational segregation _____ from 1980 to the present; at the same time, the presence of women in selected professions such as dentistry, law and engineering _____.
    a.* decreased; increased
    b. decreased; decreased
    c. increased; increased
    d. increased; decreased

CHAPTER 15
Women, Blacks, and the Labor Market

I. GENDER AND RACIAL DIFFERENCES
   A. Earnings
   B. Unemployment
   C. Occupational Distribution
   D. Education
   E. Average Earnings by Educational Attainment
   F. Related Points
       1. Nondiscriminatory Factors
       2. Interrelated Data
       3. Efficiency Loss

II. CAUSE AND EFFECT: NONDISCRIMINATORY FACTORS
   A. Rational Choice
       1. Participation and Human Capital Decisions
       2. Heterogeneous Jobs and Preferences
   B. Discrimination as a Cause
   C. A Complex Intermingling
   D. Evidence
   E. Controversy

III. ANTIDISCRIMINATION POLICIES AND ISSUES
   A. Equal Pay Act of 1963
   B. Civil Rights Act of 1964
   C. Executive Orders and Federal Contracts
   D. Comparable Worth Controversy
       1. The Concept
       2. The Debate
   E. Evidence
   F. Controversy and Conflict
       1. Free-Market View
       2. Interventionist View
   G. Have Antidiscrimination Policies Worked?

WORLD OF WORK
   1. The Gender Pay Gap: An International Comparison
   2. Discrimination in Professional Sports
   3. Women in Management: A "Mommy Track"?

LEARNING OBJECTIVES

After learning the material in Chapter 15 of *Contemporary Labor Economics*, the student should be able to:

1. compare gender and racial differences in the following key economic variables: earnings, unemployment rates, occupational distribution, educational attainment, and income

2. summarize nondiscriminatory factors that contribute to gender and racial differences in labor markets

3. show how discrimination can result in diminished national income

4. explain the extent to which observed wage differentials may be the result of rational choices

5. summarize the empirical evidence regarding discrimination against women and minorities

6. describe how the Equal Pay Act of 1963 and the Civil Rights Act of 1964 address problems of discrimination

7. discuss the various Executive Orders that address discrimination and their role in the establishment of affirmative action plans

8. evaluate the arguments in support of a comparable worth policy

9. contrast the "free-market" and "interventionist" views of anti-discrimination legislation

10. analyze the empirical evidence regarding the effectiveness of anti-discrimination legislation and policies

ANSWERS TO SELECTED END-OF-CHAPTER QUESTIONS

1. Between 1967 and 1981, the median weekly earnings of females was 61%-63% of male earnings. By 1996, the female-male earnings ratio had increased, reaching 75%. A number of factors were cited in the textbook to help explain the recent trend:
    *   Increased skill levels for female workers
    *   Perhaps discrimination has declined
    *   Restructuring of the economy away from manufacturing
    *   Decline in unionism
    *   Occupational distribution may have changed to benefit women

4. Discrimination redistributes national income by keeping women and minorities out of relatively high-wage jobs. Women and minorities are prevented from making their maximum contribution to national income.

MULTIPLE CHOICE QUESTIONS

1. In 1996 the ratio of the median weekly earnings of females to that of males was approximately:
   a. 50%-60%
   b.* 70%-80%
   c. 80%-90%
   d. 95%-100%

2. The ratio of the median weekly earnings of females to that of males:
   a. increased steadily from 1967 to the present
   b. decreased steadily from 1967 to the present
   c.* was relatively constant from 1967 to 1981, but has increased steadily since then
   d. increased steadily from 1967 to 1981, but has remained relatively constant since then

3. The largest increase in the female-male earning ratio occurred:
   a. in the 1960s
   b. in the 1970s
   c.* in the 1980s and 1990s
   d. none of the above: there has been no change in the female-male earning ratio for the past 40 years

4. In 1996 the ratio of the median weekly earnings of blacks to that of whites was approximately:
   a. 50%-60%
   b.* 70%-80%
   c. 80%-90%
   d. 95%-100%

5. The ratio of the median weekly earnings of blacks to whites:
   a. increased steadily from 1967 to the present
   b. decreased steadily from 1967 to the present
   c. was relatively constant from 1967 to 1975, but has increased steadily since then
   d.* increased from 1967 to 1975, but has modestly declined since then

6. The black-white earnings ratio is currently about:
   a. 62%   b. 69%   c.* 76%   d. 83%

7. Which one of the following is a *true* statement?
   a. Female unemployment rates are approximately twice that of males, while blacks are not overly represented among the unemployed.
   b. Women are overrepresented in blue collar jobs, and underrepresented in service and white-collar jobs
   c.* Blacks are overrepresented in the relatively low-paying blue-collar and service jobs, and underrepresented in the high-paying white-collar jobs
   d. There is little or no evidence of human-capital discrimination in the U.S.

8. Comparisons between black and white unemployment rates can be difficult because:
   a.* a larger percentage of blacks than whites have been discouraged workers
   b. among males, a larger percentage of whites than blacks have been discouraged workers
   c. the occupational distribution has been the same
   d. unemployment rates for females have consistently exceeded unemployment rates for males

9. Data on unemployment rates consistently show that the unemployment rate of:
   a. females of all races exceeds that of males of all races
   b.* blacks of both sexes exceeds that of whites of both sexes
   c. white females exceeds that of white males, but black males exceeds that of black females
   d. black females exceeds that of black males, but white males exceeds that of white females

10. High school completion rates are:
    a. lower for both females and blacks
    b. lower for females, but the same for blacks and whites
    c.* lower for blacks, but the same for males and females
    d. the same for males and females, blacks and whites

11. In 1996 the occupational distribution was:
    a.* uneven by gender and by race
    b. uneven by race but not by gender
    c. uneven by gender but not by race
    d. even by gender and by race

12. Which of the following occupations was less than 60% female in 1996?
    a.* Physicians   c. Clerical workers
    b. Retail sales workers d. Waiters and waitresses

13. In 1996, median earnings at each educational level indicate that:
    a.* white men earned more than black men and black men earned more than all women
    b. white men and white women earned more than black men
    c. white men earned more than white women, but black men earned less than black women
    d. white men earned more than black men and black men earned approximately the same as white women

14. Differences in educational attainment by gender and race:
    a.* do not explain fully earnings differences by gender and race
    b. explain fully earnings differences by gender but not by race
    c. explain fully earnings differences by race but not by gender
    d. have been eliminated

15. Labor-market discrimination creates a:
    a. redistribution of a larger GDP
    b. larger GDP but no redistribution
    c. smaller GDP but no redistribution
    d.* redistribution of a smaller GDP

16. Discrimination:
    a. redistributes national income but does not affect gross domestic product
    b. does not redistribute national income and does not affect gross domestic product
    c.* redistributes national income and reduces gross domestic product
    d. does not redistribute national income but does reduce gross domestic product

17. If eliminating racial discrimination resulted in equal unemployment rates and earnings for blacks and whites, gross domestic product would rise by approximately:
    a. less than 1%   c.* 4% – 5%
    b. 1% – 2%   d. more than 10%

18. Data comparing income by gender and race:
    a.   provide proof of discrimination when differentials are observed
    b.   provide proof of no discrimination when average salaries are equal
    c.   must be interpreted with caution because efficiency loss may be the cause of observed differentials
    d.* must be interpreted with caution because nondiscriminatory factors may explain all or part of observed differentials

19. For persons with equal educational attainment, average earnings may be different due to factors other than discrimination. Which of the following is *not* a non-discriminatory factor which can explain wage differentials?
    a.   Participation decisions   c.* Homogeneous jobs
    b.   Human capital decisions   d.   Heterogeneous preferences

20. Which one of the following is *not* a nondiscriminatory factor contributing to earnings differences?
    a.   rational choice in participation and human capital decisions
    b.   heterogeneous preferences
    c.* participation decisions in response to sexual harassment in the workplace
    d.   differences in job characteristics

21. Critics of the "rational choice" argument contend that:
    a.   differences in earnings may be the result of freely-made schooling and occupational choices
    b.* differences in schooling and occupational choices are caused by discrimination
    c.   wage differentials may be due to nondiscriminatory factors
    d.   sexual harassment and discrimination do not affect occupational choices

22. According to empirical estimates, approximately what proportion of the observed female-male earnings gap and black-white earnings gap can be explained by nondiscriminatory factors?
    a.   none   c.* more than half
    b.   no more than half   d.   virtually all

23. Studies by Blau and Kahn report that productivity differences "explain" approximately:
    a.* two-thirds of the wage difference for women and nine-tenths for blacks
    b.   half of the wage difference for both women and blacks
    c.   one-third of the wage difference for women and one-tenth for blacks
    d.   one-quarter of the wage difference for women and half for blacks

24. Empirical estimates of the extent of discrimination may be *upwardly* biased if:
    a.* certain variables which have a positive effect on productivity are omitted from the study
    b.   certain variables which have a negative effect on productivity are omitted from the study
    c.   many of the control variables (such as education or occupation) reflect discriminatory decisions
    d.   all of the above

25. Empirical estimates of the extent of discrimination may be *downwardly* biased if:
    a.   certain variables which have a positive effect on productivity are omitted from the study
    b.*   certain variables which have a negative effect on productivity are omitted from the study
    c.   many of the control variables (such as education or occupation) reflect personal choices
    d.   all of the above

26. The Equal Pay Act of 1963 was of little help to many women because:
    a.*   it did not address occupational segregation
    b.   male employers ignored the act because it provided no enforcement power
    c.   the act addressed only racial discrimination, not discrimination based on gender
    d.   it was declared unconstitutional and later replaced by the Civil Rights Act

27. Which of the following required firms holding federal contracts to establish "affirmative action" programs?
    a.   Equal Pay Act of 1963   c.*   A 1968 Executive Order
    b.   Civil Rights Act of 1964   d.   Landrum-Griffin Act of 1959

28. Which of the following required equal treatment for all persons in hiring, firing, promotion and compensation decisions?
    a.   Equal Pay Act of 1963   c.   A 1968 Executive Order
    b.*   Civil Rights Act of 1964   d.   Landrum-Griffin Act of 1959

29. Two jobs are said to be of "comparable worth" if:
    a.   they would pay the same wage rate in the absence of occupational segregation
    b.   society views the jobs as creating the same value of marginal product
    c.   they pay the same wage rate
    d.*   the knowledge, skills, effort, and working conditions in the jobs are comparable

30. Which of the following is most consistent with the comparable worth doctrine?
    a.*   Persons with similar knowledge, skills, effort, and working conditions should receive the same pay
    b.   Workers should be paid an amount equal to the value of their marginal products
    c.   Workers in different jobs should be paid equally
    d.   Workers should receive the same pay if they do the same work

31. Which one of the following views of the labor market best represents the views of *opponents* of comparable worth?
    a.   Labor markets are not competitive
    b.*   Wage rates reflect marginal products
    c.   Wage rates are determined by custom, tradition and discrimination
    d.   There are no economic incentives in labor markets

32. Which one of the following views of the labor market best represents the views of *proponents* of comparable worth?
    a.   Labor markets are competitive
    b.   Wage rates reflect marginal products
    c.*   Market wages are distorted by unions, statistical discrimination, and imperfect information
    d.   Policies aimed to aid disadvantaged groups often do not aid such groups

33. At firms obligated to undertake affirmative action, female and minority shares of employment:
    a.   grew consistently from 1975 to the present
    b.*   grew from 1975 to 1980, but have not changed appreciably since then
    c.   did not change appreciably from 1965 to 1975, but have grown consistently since then
    d.   did not change from 1965 to the present

34. Empirical evidence indicates that affirmative action programs in the 1970s:
    a.   improved employment opportunities for minorities but not women
    b.   improved employment opportunities for women but not minorities
    c.   failed to improve employment opportunities for both women and minorities
    d.*   improved employment opportunities for minorities and for women

35. According to Milton Friedman, current government anti-discrimination policies:
    a.   are insufficient because they do not correct the effects of past discrimination
    b.   attack only the demand side of the labor market, while the problem is that not enough qualified women and minority workers are available for high-paying jobs
    c.   are insufficient because seniority rules and other union hiring practices must be eliminated before women and minorities can be expected to achieve the same status as white males
    d.*   are unnecessary since competition forces firms to separate differences in productivity from other personal worker characteristics

36. (*World of Work* 15-1) Francine Blau and Lawrence Kahn have reported that the gender pay gap is larger in the United States than in some other countries—such as Sweden, Norway, and Australia—because:
    a.   American women tend to have less education than women in other countries
    b.   Historically, the U.S. has not been committed to equal pay for women than have other countries
    c.   There is a relatively small gap in pay between low- and high-skilled workers in the U.S. and women are disproportionately represented in lower-skilled jobs
    d.*   There is a relatively large gap in pay between low- and high-skilled workers in the U.S. and women are disproportionately represented in low-skilled jobs

37. (*World of Work* 15-2) Many studies of discrimination have been undertaken for professional sports. Which of the following is *not* a conclusion reached in this body of sports discrimination research?
    a.   Controlling for nondiscriminatory factors (such as experience and performance), black players do not earn less than white players in professional basketball
    b.   Team customers are a source of discrimination in professional basketball
    c.*   Characteristics of metropolitan areas are not a source of earnings differentials in professional baseball
    d.   There is segregation among player positions in professional football

38. (*World of Work* 15-3) Felice Schwartz has proposed that one approach to the problem of reduced labor force growth in the next decade is for managers to:
    a.   not distinguish between different "types" of women managers
    b.*   provide additional job flexibility for women who wish to manage both career and family
    c.   provide additional on-the-job training to women and minorities
    d.   increase the wages paid to women and minorities to attract them from alternative uses of their time

CHAPTER 16
Job Search: External and Internal

I.   INTRODUCTION

II.   EXTENDED JOB SEARCH
    A.   Inflation and Job Search
         1.   Expected Inflation
         2.   Unexpected Inflation
    B.   Unemployment Compensation and Job Search
    C.   Other Implications of the Search Model
    D.   Empirical Evidence

III. INTERNAL LABOR MARKETS
    A.   Characteristics of Internal Labor Markets
    B.   Reasons for Internal Labor Markets
         1.   Advantages to Employers
         2.   Advantages to Workers
    C.   The Role of Unions
    D.   Labor Allocation and the Wage Structure
    E.   The Efficiency Issue

WORLD OF WORK
         1.   How Do the Unemployed Search for Work?
         2.   Long-Term Jobs in the U.S. Economy

GLOBAL PERSPECTIVE
         1.   Job Tenure, 1995

LEARNING OBJECTIVES

After learning the material in Chapter 16 of *Contemporary Labor Economics*, the student should be able to:

1.   distinguish internal job search from external job search

2.   explain why both workers and employers search for the best match

3.   cite the costs and benefits of job search

4.   describe the impact of both expected and unexpected inflation on expected job search duration

5.   derive and discuss several implications of the job search model

6.   review empirical findings on acceptance wages and job search duration

7.   describe the characteristics of internal labor markets and cite their advantages to both firms and workers

8.   summarize how an internal labor market affects labor allocation and the wage structure

9.   contrast static and dynamic efficiency and describe the impact of internal labor markets on both.

ANSWERS TO SELECTED END-OF-CHAPTER QUESTIONS

1. A rate of inflation below the expected rate will decrease the probability that a job searcher will accept the next wage offer and thus increase the expected length of the workers unemployment spell. A decrease in unemployment benefits will have the opposite effect.

MULTIPLE CHOICE QUESTIONS

1. Which of the following is *not* typically given as a reason for job search?
    a.   Workers are heterogeneous
    b.   Information is imperfect
    c.   Firms' compensation packages differ from one another
    d.* Firms are homogeneous

2. The model of job search given in the text assumes that workers can estimate all but which of the following:
    a.   the shape of the wage offer distribution
    b.   the approximate mean of the wage offer distribution
    c.* the approximate value of any given wage offer
    d.   the variance of the wage offer distribution

3. An unemployed worker will continue a job search providing the:
    a.   expected benefit of continued search is rising
    b.   expected cost of continued search is falling
    c.* last wage offer was below the acceptance wage
    d.   worker is able to "store" job offers

4. The *major* cost of continued job search is:
    a.   the cost of placing job-wanted advertisements in the newspaper
    b.   expenses paid to a job-placement agency
    c.* foregone wages of job offers not accepted
    d.   transportation expenses of going to job interviews

Questions 5 – 7 refer to the following graph, which shows the probability distribution of wage offers for Sally, who is currently unemployed and searching for a job:

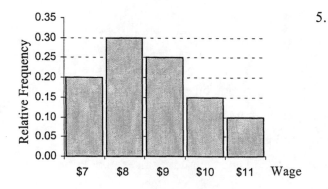

5. If $8.50 is the acceptance wage, what is the probability of Sally finding her next wage offer acceptable?

a.	.25	c.*	.50
b.	.30	d.	.70

6. If the rate of inflation increases but Sally mistakenly believes it has not, then:
   a. both the acceptance wage and the entire distribution will shift to the left, thereby leaving expected search duration unchanged
   b. the acceptance wage will shift to the right, thereby reducing excepted search duration
   c.* the entire distribution will shift to the right, but the acceptance wage will not, thereby reducing expected search duration
   d. both the acceptance wage and the entire distribution will shift to the right, thereby leaving expected search duration unchanged

7. If Sally correctly anticipates an increase in the rate of inflation, then:
   a. both the acceptance wage and the entire distribution will shift to the left, thereby leaving expected search duration unchanged
   b. the acceptance wage will shift to the right, thereby reducing expected search duration
   c. the entire distribution will shift to the right, but the acceptance wage will not, thereby reducing expected search duration
   d.* both the acceptance wage and the entire distribution will shift to the right, thereby leaving expected search duration unchanged

8. The probability of accepting the next wage offer is:
   a. higher, the higher is the acceptance wage
   b. lower, the lower is the acceptance wage
   c.* lower, the higher is the acceptance wage
   d. higher, the higher is unemployment compensation

9. A fully anticipated reduction in the rate of inflation will:
   a. reduce the unemployment rate in the short run, but not in the long run
   b. reduce the unemployment rate in the both the short run and the long run
   c. increase the unemployment rate in the short run, but not in the long run
   d.* have very little impact on the unemployment rate in either the short run or the long run

10. An unanticipated reduction in the rate of inflation will:
    a. reduce the unemployment rate in the short run, but not in the long run
    b. reduce the unemployment rate in the both the short run and the long run
    c.* increase the unemployment rate in the short run, but not in the long run
    d. have very little impact on the unemployment rate in either the short run or the long run

11. An increase in unemployment compensation is predicted to:
    a. reduce unemployment by raising acceptance wage rates
    b. reduce unemployment by reducing acceptance wage rates
    c. increase unemployment by reducing acceptance wage rates
    d.* increase unemployment by raising acceptance wage rates

12. In addition to their regular unemployment benefits, a recent Washington state program offered an average of $562 to any job loser who became reemployed *within 13 weeks of filing for unemployment compensation*. Economic theory suggests that such a "bounty" scheme should:
    a. reduce job search duration by shifting the wage offer distribution to the left
    b.* reduce job search duration by decreasing the acceptance wage and intensifying job search
    c. reduce job search duration by shifting the wage offer distribution to the right
    d. have no effect on job search duration, as the acceptance wage will decrease to offset the effect of the shifting wage offer distribution

13. A recent tax reform made all unemployment compensation subject to the income tax. Since this compensation was tax free prior to the reform, this policy change likely:
    a.   reduced average job search duration and increased the unemployment rate
    b.   increased average job search duration and increased the unemployment rate
    c.   increased acceptance wages and decreased the unemployment rate
    d.*   reduced acceptance wages and decreased the unemployment rate

14. The job search model implies that:
    a.   the longer the expected job tenure, the lower the acceptance wage
    b.   the higher the acceptance wage, the shorter the expected search duration
    c.*   expected search duration is longer during a recession
    d.   if job searchers perceive that a recession is temporary, they will reduce their acceptance wages

15. The longer the expected length of tenure on the job:
    a.*   the higher the acceptance wage and the longer the expected job search duration
    b.   the higher the acceptance wage and the shorter the expected job search duration
    c.   the lower the acceptance wage and the longer the expected job search duration
    d.   the lower the acceptance wage and the shorter the expected job search duration

16. Which of the following contributes to a higher unemployment rate of black youths compared to white youths?
    a.   Both wage offer distributions and acceptance wages are lower for black youths
    b.   The black wage offer distribution is to the right of the white distribution
    c.   White youths have a higher acceptance wage than black youths
    d.*   Black youths have a higher acceptance wage than white youths

17. Which of the following is *not* a characteristic of an internal labor market?
    a.   A port of entry, at which workers gain access to the bottom of the job ladder
    b.   A hierarchy of jobs constituting the job ladder
    c.   A set of rules and procedures governing the wage structure
    d.*   The appointment of a new company president who has little or no tenure at the firm

18. Which one of the following is associated with an internal labor market?
    a.   Port of entry disconnected from an external labor market
    b.   Port of entry at the top of the job ladder
    c.*   Port of entry at the bottom of the job ladder
    d.   The absence of a job hierarchy

19. Wage rates are most likely to be set in accordance with administrative rules and procedures in the:
    a.   secondary labor market   c.   external labor market
    b.*   internal labor market   d.   orthodox labor market

20. Internal labor markets are most likely to exist if:
    a.   workers do not require extensive amounts of firm-specific training
    b.*   there are substantial costs to the employer associated with worker turnover
    c.   costs of screening and recruiting job applicants are relatively low
    d.   workers' productivity does not increase with experience

21.   Internal labor markets are likely to occur when:
       a.   principal-agent problems are absent
       b.   firms expect a high rate of turnover and low hiring costs
       c.   workers at a particular firm require general training
       d.*   workers at a particular firm require specific training

22.   Which of the following is *not* a benefit to employers of an internal labor market?
       a.   A greater return from investments in specific training
       b.*   A greater return from investment in general training
       c.   A solution to a principal-agent problem
       d.   Greater employee identification with the firm's objectives

23.   Internal labor markets benefit workers in that such markets:
       a.*   provide job security and opportunities for advancement
       b.   allow wage rates to adapt quickly to changing economic conditions
       c.   provide increased mobility from one firm to another as a method of career advancement
       d.   pay for workers' general training

24.   Internal labor markets benefit senior employees by:
       a.   forcing the firm to pay all of the expenses associated with general training
       b.   providing them with greater freedom through the informal work rules associated with
             such markets
       c.*   providing them with increased protection from job layoff
       d.   protecting them from pay cuts when they leave the firm for other jobs

25.   An internal labor market is:
       a.*   conducive to unionization because high levels of specific training endow workers with
             substantial bargaining power
       b.   conducive to unionization because unions are highly demanded by workers in firms
             characterized by high turnover
       c.   at odds with unionization because unions find it difficult to organize workers in firms
             characterized by high turnover
       d.   at odds with unionization because workers and firms with such markets form a symbiotic
             relationship without the need for unions

26.   In an internal labor market, promotions are generally accorded on the basis of:
       a.   ability   c.*   seniority
       b.   work effort   d.   age

27.   Suppose a management team assigns 100 points to the job of clerk/typist and 75 points to a job on
       the loading dock. If the wage paid to a clerk/typist is $8.00 per hour, then the hourly wage paid
       to a worker on the loading dock would be:
       a. $2   b.* $6   c. $8   d. $10

28.   Because workers in internal labor markets are promoted on the basis of seniority:
       a.   such markets are allocatively inefficient because seniority takes precedence over ability
       b.*   dynamic efficiency is enhanced by removing a disincentive for older workers to pass
             along skills to younger workers
       c.   static efficiency is enhanced by allocating the most able workers to each job
       d.   some other scheme must be introduced, such as tournament pay, to improve efficiency in
             such markets

29. Internal labor markets may contribute to dynamic efficiency by:
    a. paying younger workers more than their marginal revenue products
    b.* paying older workers more than their marginal revenue products
    c. paying older workers less than their marginal revenue products
    d. paying each worker a wage equal to her marginal revenue product

30. (*World of Work* 16-1) The most common method of job search is:
    a. using a public or private employment agency
    b. sending out a resume
    c. placing or answering a want-ad
    d.* contacting an employer directly

31. (*World of Work* 16-2) According to research by Robert E. Hall, more than half of U.S. workers:
    a.* were employed in jobs which would last at least five years
    b. were employed in jobs which would last less than five years
    c. were employed in jobs which would last at least fifteen years
    d. changed jobs within the past three years

CHAPTER 17
The Personal Distribution of Earnings

GLOBAL PERSPECTIVE
1.   Earnings Mobility, 1986 – 1991
2.   Male Earnings Inequality

LEARNING OBJECTIVES

After learning the material in Chapter 17 of *Contemporary Labor Economics*, the student should be able to:

1.   correctly identify the mean, median, and mode from a frequency distribution of earnings

2.   describe the U.S. distribution of earnings and draw a frequency distribution that approximates its shape

3.   plot a Lorenz curve from earnings distribution data and estimate the Gini coefficient from its shape and position

4.   explain, with reference to the human capital model, how both formal education and on-the-job training relate to the earnings distribution

5.   outline the multi-factor approach to the earnings distribution

6.   specify those factors that contribute to differences in earnings, and diagram them schematically

7.   explain why the earnings distribution is skewed to the right

8.   list and describe the basic types of mobility within the earnings distribution

9.   specify and evaluate the reasons given for the increase in earnings inequality

ANSWERS TO SELECTED END-OF-CHAPTER QUESTIONS

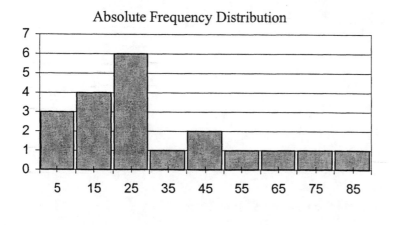

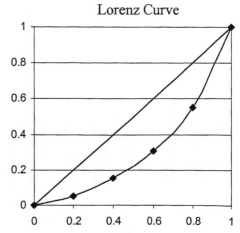

1.   a.   The mode is between $20,000 and $30,000.
                The mean is $31,000.
                The median is $23,500.

b.   The cumulative distribution of earnings is as follows:
   Lowest 20%   4.8%
   Lowest 40%   15.5
   Lowest 60%   30.8
   Lowest 80%   55.2
   Total: 100.0%

5.   The transfers may reduce work hours of low-earnings workers, thereby aggravating the inequality of annual earnings.

MULTIPLE CHOICE QUESTIONS

Questions 1-4 refer to the following diagram which shows the earnings distribution for a small hypothetical economy (all figures in thousands).

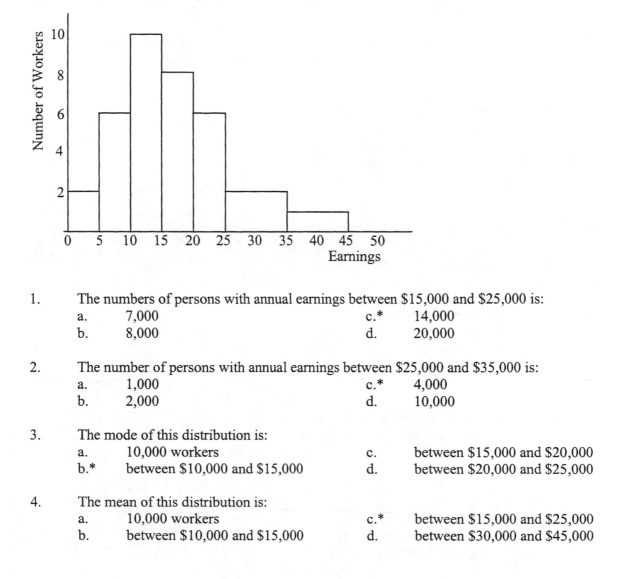

1.   The numbers of persons with annual earnings between $15,000 and $25,000 is:
   a.   7,000   c.*   14,000
   b.   8,000   d.   20,000

2.   The number of persons with annual earnings between $25,000 and $35,000 is:
   a.   1,000   c.*   4,000
   b.   2,000   d.   10,000

3.   The mode of this distribution is:
   a.   10,000 workers   c.   between $15,000 and $20,000
   b.* between $10,000 and $15,000 d.   between $20,000 and $25,000

4.   The mean of this distribution is:
   a.   10,000 workers   c.*   between $15,000 and $25,000
   b.   between $10,000 and $15,000 d.   between $30,000 and $45,000

5.   The U.S. earnings distribution is:
     a.   best represented by a straight line Lorenz curve
     b.*   not symmetrical around the mean earnings level
     c.   concentrated around a rightward mode
     d.   skewed to the left

6.   The U.S. earnings distribution is:
     a.   skewed toward lower earnings   c.   symmetrical
     b.*   skewed toward higher earnings   d.   uniform

7.   Which of the following is a *true* statement regarding the U.S. earnings distribution?
     a.*   Because the distribution is skewed to the right, the mean exceeds the mode
     b.   Because the distribution is skewed to the right, the mode exceeds the mean
     c.   Because the distribution is skewed to the left, the mean exceeds the mode
     d.   Because the distribution is skewed to the left, the mode exceeds the median

8.   For the U.S. earnings distribution, the:
     a.*   mode is less than the median   c.   mean is less than the median
     b.   median is greater than the mean   d.   mode is greater than the mean

9.   If all workers received the same earnings:
     a.*   the Gini coefficient of earnings would be 1
     b.   the Gini coefficient of earnings would be 0
     c.   the earnings distribution would have a normal bell-shaped appearance
     d.   the Lorenz curve would be skewed to the left

Question 10 and 11 refer to the diagram at right:

10. If an increase in the minimum wage increases the
     earnings of low-income individuals relative to high-
     income individuals, this will cause the Lorenz curve
     to shift from:
     a.   A to B and the Gini coefficient will rise
     b.   A to B and the Gini coefficient will fall
     c.   B to A and the Gini coefficient will rise
     d.*   B to A and the Gini coefficient will fall

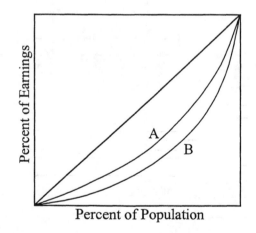

11. An increase in earnings inequality would be shown by a:
     a.*   shift from line A to line B   c.   movement up to the right along line A
     b.   shift from lime B to line A   d.   movement down to the left along line A

12. If an increase in the sales tax reduces the earnings of low-income individuals relative to high-
     income individuals, this would:
     a.   cause the Gini coefficient to fall
     b.*   cause the Gini coefficient to rise
     c.   leave the Gini coefficient unchanged
     d.   move the Lorenz curve closer to the diagonal

140

Questions 13 and 14 refer to the following quintile earnings distribution data:

Quintile	Percent
Lowest 20%	4%
Second 20%	11%
Third 20%	16%
Fourth 20%	24%
Highest 20%	45%

13. If one were to draw a Lorenz curve from the data, what point would be plotted corresponding to "80%" on the horizontal axis?
   a.   11%   c.   45%
   b.   24%   d.* 55%

14. The median of this distribution is in the:
   a.   second 20%   c.* fourth 20%
   b.   third 20%   d.   highest 20%

15. The Gini coefficient measures:
   a.   the area under the Lorenz curve
   b.   the area above the Lorenz curve
   c.* twice the area between the Lorenz curve and the line of equality
   d.   half the area between the Lorenz curve and the line of equality

16. If earnings inequality continues to increase, the Lorenz curve will shift:
   a.* away from the diagonal and the Gini coefficient will rise
   b.   away from the diagonal and the Gini coefficient will fall
   c.   toward the diagonal and the Gini coefficient will rise
   d.   towards the diagonal and the Gini coefficient will fall

17. Which one of the following is a *true* statement?
   a.* The earnings distribution for full-time workers is less skewed than the one for all workers
   b.   When fringe benefits are included, the earnings distribution narrows
   c.   The distribution of income is no different from the distribution of earnings
   d.   The Lorenz curve indicates the extent of personal movement within the distribution of earnings

18. Including fringe benefits with earnings, the Lorenz curve moves:
   a.* away from the diagonal and the Gini coefficient rises
   b.   away from the diagonal and the Gini coefficient falls
   c.   toward the diagonal and the Gini coefficient rises
   d.   toward the diagonal and the Gini coefficient falls

19. The basic human capital model predicts that:
   a.* the greater are the differences in the quantity and quality of training, the greater is the inequality of earnings.
   b.   the greater the length and quality of one's formal training, the higher will be the investment costs and the lower will be expected earnings
   c.   the earnings distribution will be symmetric
   d.   the Gini coefficient will eventually become zero

20. Econometric studies that hold other factors constant show that:
   a.* there is a positive relationship between education and earnings
   b.   there is no relationship between education and earnings
   c.   there is no relationship between the quality of education and earnings
   d.   formal schooling explains most of the differences in individual earnings

141

21. The multifactor explanation of the distribution of earnings typically *excludes*:
    a.   innate ability   c.*   non-monetary returns to training
    b.   family background   d.   risk-taking and chance

22. Those persons with greater amounts of formal education tend to have:
    a.   less on-the-job training, which increases the skewness of the earnings distribution
    b.   less on-the-job training, which decreases the skewness of the earnings distribution
    c.*   more on-the-job training, which increases the skewness of the earnings distribution
    d.   more on-the-job training, which decreases the skewness of the earnings distribution

23. Which of the following factors does *not* help explain why the earnings distribution is skewed to the right?
    a.   Family background
    b.   Discrimination
    c.   The impact of ability on human capital decisions
    d.*   Churning within the distribution

24. If persons of greater ability also tend to invest more in human capital, then the impact of human capital on earnings will be:
    a.   understated   c.   unaffected
    b.*   overstated   d.   a direct impact

25. If the various elements of innate ability are positively correlated and interact with one another multiplicatively rather than additively to determine earnings, then:
    a.*   the distribution of earnings will tend to be more skewed to the right
    b.   the distribution of earnings will tend to be more skewed to the left
    c.   the distribution of earnings will shift to the left
    d.   the total demand for training will tend to fall

26. Family background is thought to influence an individual's earnings:
    a.   directly, but not through any indirect effects on human capital decisions
    b.*   directly, and indirectly through greater investments in human capital
    c.   indirectly through greater investments in human capital, but not directly
    d.   directly, and indirectly through its impact on discrimination

27. Discrimination contributes to earnings inequality through:
    a.   pay discrimination only
    b.   pay discrimination and occupational segregation only
    c.*   pay discrimination, occupational segregation, and human capital discrimination
    d.   chance and risk taking, which reduce the Gini coefficient

28. According to empirical evidence, there is _____ mobility within the earnings distribution; the distribution of annual earnings is _____ unequal than the distribution of lifetime earnings.
    a.   little; more   c.*   substantial; more
    b.   little; less   d.   substantial; less

29. The 90 – 10 ratio (the wage at the 90th percentile divided by the 10th percentile wage) shows:
    a.*   increasing inequality among men and women from 1973 to 1996
    b.   increasing inequality among men from 1973 to 1979, but reduced inequality since then
    c.   increasing inequality for men but not for women since 1973
    d.   increasing inequality for women but not for men since 1973

30. Which of the following is *not* an explanation advanced to explain the increase in earnings inequality?
    a. Deindustrialization
    b. Import competition and the decline of unionism
    c. Demographic changes
    d.* Decreased demand for skilled labor

31. Evidence indicates that most of the growth in earnings inequality since 1970 is:
    a.* within each age group and within each industry
    b. within each age group and between industries
    c. between age groups and within each industry
    d. between age groups and between industries

32. The distribution of earnings has become more unequal:
    a. among women but not among men
    b. due to the reduction in the college wage premium in the 1980s
    c.* in part due to greater import competition in the 1980s
    d. due to a reduction in the number of young and inexperienced workers in the 1990s

33. (*World of Work* 17-1) Research by Gottschalk and Moffit shows that recent increases in year-to-year variations in earnings:
    a. were concentrated among those with the highest incomes
    b. were concentrated among those with the highest education
    c.* can account for up to half of the increase in earnings inequality over the period
    d. have moderated the increase in earnings inequality over the period

34. (*World of Work* 17-2) Compared to the private sector, the public sector earnings distribution tends to be:
    a. more unequal because government workers tend to be employed in service occupations
    b. more unequal because government pay scales are generally higher
    c. less unequal because of the relatively large number of management positions in government
    d.* less unequal because blue-collar employees are generally paid more and white-collar employees are generally paid less than their private-sector counterparts

CHAPTER 18
Labor Productivity:
Wages, Prices, and Employment

LEARNING OBJECTIVES

After learning the material in Chapter 18 of *Contemporary Labor Economics*, the student should be able to:

1. explain the concept of productivity and describe how it is measured

2. list the strengths and weaknesses of the BLS Productivity Index as a measure of productivity

3. graphically derive and explain the relationship between productivity growth and the growth of real wage rates for the economy as a whole

4. describe the process by which productivity increases may offset the inflationary impacts of nominal wage increases

5. list and discuss the basic causes of long-term productivity growth

6. explain why labor productivity displays a procyclical pattern

7. analyze how price and income elasticities of demand affect the relationship between productivity growth and employment growth in a specific industry

8. cite several factors that contributed to the slowdown in productivity growth over the past three decades

ANSWERS TO SELECTED END-OF-CHAPTER QUESTIONS

2. Year 1: Productivity Index = 88.9.
    Year 2: Productivity Index = 100.0;
        Rate of productivity growth = 12.5%.
    Year 3: Productivity Index = 111.1;
        Rate of productivity growth = 11.1%.

6. Each would rise approximately 3%.

9. If increases in nominal wages are greater than improvements in productivity, unit labor costs will rise, which creates pressure for prices to rise. All else constant—particularly demand changes—higher productivity growth will lead to greater employment growth in an industry.

10. Given the assumption, industry X will decline: its unit labor costs will rise and product demand is price elastic and income inelastic.

MULTIPLE CHOICE QUESTIONS

1. Labor productivity is best defined as:
    a.   real GDP divided by unit labor costs
    b.   nominal GDP divided by the number of worker hours
    c.   nominal GDP divided by labor costs
    d.* real GDP divided by the number of worker hours

2. If real GDP falls by 2% while work hours fall by 10%, then labor productivity:
    a.   falls
    b.   is unchanged
    c.* rises
    d.   might fall, but we cannot know without more information

3. Suppose productivity stood at 5.00 in 1998, and 5.25 in 1999. If 1998 is the base year, the productivity *index* for 1999 is:
   a. 0.25   b. 5   c.* 105   d. 125

4. Labor productivity in the base year was 20. The following year, the productivity index stood at 105. Labor productivity in the second year was:
   a. 5   b. 20   c.* 21   d. 105

5. One shortcoming of the Bureau of Labor Statistics Index of Productivity is that it:
   a. overstates the importance of capital investments
   b. fails to include part-time workers
   c. double counts public sector output
   d.* ignores changes in the quality of output

6. The secular increase in real wages resulted from increases in labor productivity:
   a.* that have increased the demand for labor faster than the supply of labor
   b. that have increased the supply of labor faster than the demand for labor
   c. that have decreased the demand for labor faster than the supply of labor
   d. made possible by increased public sector output

7. If nominal wages rose 1.5% and productivity increased 3% in a given year, we should expect:
   a. an increase in unit labor costs and upward pressure on prices
   b. an increase in unit labor costs and downward pressure on prices
   c. a decrease in unit labor costs and upward pressure on prices
   d.* a decrease in unit labor costs and downward pressure on prices

8. Which one of the following wage-productivity combinations will place the greatest upward pressure on the price level?
   a. Nominal wage increase of 5%, productivity increase of 5%
   b.* Nominal wage increase of 4%, productivity increase of 2%
   c. Nominal wage decrease of 5%, productivity increase of 5%
   d. Nominal wage increase of 2%, productivity increase of 4%

9. Which one of the following most closely corresponds to the average annual rate of productivity growth in the United States over the past century?
   a. 0-1%   b.* 2-3%   c. 4-5%   d. 6-7%

10. Productivity growth:
    a. has been steady since 1960
    b.* was greater in the 1960s than the 1980s
    c. was very erratic in the 1960s but increased consistently during the 1970s
    d. has consistently exceeded 2% per year in the 1990s

11. According to evidence reported by Edward F. Denison, the most important source of rising productivity over the period 1929 – 1982 was:
    a. increased average quality of labor
    b. increased quantity of physical capital
    c.* increased efficiency
    d. increased nominal wages

12. According to evidence reported by Edward F. Denison, which of the following *restricted* productivity growth over the period 1929 – 1982?
   a.   Changes in the capital-labor ratio
   b.   Diseconomies of scale and scope
   c.*   Increased regulations placed on businesses
   d.   Reductions in workplace safety

13. The average quality of labor has increased, partly because the demand for education and health care are:
   a.*   income elastic—rising national income generates more than proportional increases in spending on these items
   b.   income elastic—falling national income generates more than proportional increases in spending on these items
   c.   income inelastic—rising national income generates more than proportional increases in spending on these items
   d.   income inelastic—rising national income generates less than proportional increases in spending on these items

14. Which of the following is one of the reasons typically given for the relatively high secular growth in productivity for the period 1889 – 1969?
   a.*   A three-fold increase in the capital-labor ratio
   b.   An increase in service sector output relative to the manufacturing sector
   c.   An increase in the average length of the workweek
   d.   An increase in the use of quotas and tariffs to protect domestic industries

15. Which of the following is not considered a source of increased labor efficiency?
   a.   Technological progress
   b.   Reallocation of labor from less to more productive uses
   c.   Changes in society's institutional and cultural setting and resulting public policies
   d.*   Increases in the capital-labor ratio

16. For the 1889 – 1969 period in the U.S., the rate of productivity growth in years of declining real output was:
   a.*   negative
   b.   positive
   c.   faster than in years of expanding real output
   d.   similar to that in years of expanding real output

17. Productivity appears to be:
   a.*   procyclical; firms are reluctant to lay off workers in a recession, so output falls more than employment
   b.   procyclical; firms are quick to lay off workers in a recession, so employment falls more than output
   c.   countercyclical; firms are reluctant to lay off workers in a recession, so output falls more than employment
   d.   countercyclical; firms are quick to lay off workers in a recession, so employment falls more than output

18. Empirical evidence reported by John Kendrick indicates that productivity growth tends to be _____ as the economy expands and _____ as real output declines.
    a.   positive; positive   c.   negative; positive
    b.*   positive; negative   d.   negative; negative

19. Productivity growth:
    a.*   falls below its trend rate in a recession and rises above it in an expansion
    b.   rises above its trend rate in a recession and falls below it in an expansion
    c.   is counter-cyclical
    d.   is independent of the business cycle

20. Productivity declines may worsen recessions by causing unit labor costs:
    a.*   to rise, thereby resulting in falling profits and lower investment spending
    b.   to rise, thereby resulting in greater retained earnings by firms
    c.   to fall, thereby creating incentives for government intervention
    d.   to fall, thereby reducing consumer spending power

21. Which of the following best describes the relationship between productivity changes and investment during a recession?
    a.   Unit labor costs rise, plant and equipment are utilized more, investment rises
    b.   Unit labor costs fall, plant and equipment are utilized more, investment rises
    c.   Unit labor costs fall, plant and equipment are utilized less, investment rises
    d.*   Unit labor costs rise, plant and equipment are utilized less, investment falls

22. An economy-wide increase in productivity caused by improved technology would most likely:
    a.   increase unemployment, because any given output could be produced with less labor
    b.   increase inflation, thereby decreasing profits and investment
    c.   increase output, but decrease employment
    d.*   increase real incomes, thereby increasing aggregate demand and reducing unemployment

23. Productivity growth:
    a.   has been associated with rising aggregate unemployment
    b.*   has been associated with growing aggregate employment
    c.   in specific industries has been associated with growing employment in those industries
    d.   in specific industries has been associated with growing unemployment in those industries

24. Wage rates tend to change with national rather than with industry productivity because:
    a.   the minimum wage and other government controls prevent industry wage differentials
    b.   productivity differences result in product price differences, leaving real wages unchanged
    c.*   labor supply responses tend to prevent wages from diverging in the various industries
    d.   labor demand responses tend to prevent wages from diverging in the various industries

25. Suppose demand conditions in industries X and Y are identical but that productivity increases by 5% in industry X and 2% in industry Y. If economy-wide productivity and the average wage each rise by 3%, we should expect that:
    a.*   output and employment in X will increase relative to Y
    b.   output and employment in X and Y will not change relative to one another, since wages will increase by 5% in X and 2% in Y
    c.   output and employment in Y will increase relative to X
    d.   no statement can be made concerning output and employment in either industry without more information

26. Suppose productivity increases by 5% in industry X and 2% in industry Y. Further suppose the demand for X has fallen while the demand for Y has increased. If economy-wide productivity and the average wage each rise by 3%, we should expect that:
   a. output and employment in X will increase relative to Y
   b. output and employment in X and Y will not change relative to one another, since wages will increase by 5% in X and 2% in Y
   c. output and employment in Y will increase relative to X
   d.* no statement can be made concerning output and employment in either industry without more information

27. Suppose that an economy's real wages and its average productivity are both increasing at a 2% annual rate. Further assume that productivity in industry X is growing at a 4% annual rate. Under what conditions might output and employment in industry X *fall*?
   a. Price-elastic product demand
   b. Price-inelastic product demand
   c.* The output of industry X is an inferior good
   d. The output of industry X is a normal good

28. Higher than average productivity growth in industry X would *least* likely lead to relative employment growth in industry X if the demand for X is:
   a.* both price and income inelastic
   b. both price and income elastic
   c. price inelastic and income elastic
   d. price elastic and income elastic

29. Under what conditions would we expect to find the greatest growth of output and employment in a specific industry?
   a.* High productivity growth, price-elastic product demand, income-elastic product demand
   b. High productivity growth, price-elastic product demand, income-inelastic product demand
   c. Low productivity growth, price-inelastic product demand, income-inelastic product demand
   d. High productivity growth, price-inelastic product demand, income-elastic product demand

30. Which one of the following most closely corresponds to the average annual rate of productivity growth in the U.S. for the period 1948 – 1973?
   a. 0-1%   b. 1-2%   c.* 2-4%   d. 5-8%

31. Which one of the following most closely corresponds to the average annual rate of productivity growth in the U.S. for the period 1973 – 1997?
   a. 0-1%   b.* 1-2%   c. 2-4%   d. 5-8%

32. Which one of the following did *not* contribute to the productivity slowdown of the past 25 years?
   a. Rapid expansion of the labor force
   b. Reductions in spending on research and development
   c. Increased governmental regulation
   d.* Increased spending on the nation's infrastructure that detracted from private investment spending

33. One possible "institutional" explanation for the recent U.S. productivity slowdown is that:
    a. U.S. investment in capital goods has risen relative to other developed countries
    b.* U.S. industrial relations are characterized by an adversarial relationship between workers and managers
    c. the composition of investment spending in the U.S. shifted toward research and development and away from heavy machinery
    d. low marginal tax rates on U.S. businesses reduced their incentives to invest in physical capital

34. (*World of Work* 18-1) Empirical studies of the productivity of public capital indicate:
    a. a consensus that public capital is approximately half as productive as private capital
    b. a consensus that public capital is approximately twice as productive as private capital
    c.* high productivity when using national data, but low productivity using state and regional data
    d. high productivity when using state and regional data, but low productivity using national data

35. (*World of Work* 18-2) Which of the following may help to explain why measured productivity has increased more in manufacturing than in services in recent years?
    a.* It is comparatively difficult to substitute capital for labor in service industries
    b. The influx of women into the labor force has kept manufacturing wages relatively low
    c. Service industries have had to hire relatively high-wage, high-skilled workers, since technological innovation in manufacturing has created relatively many low-wage jobs
    d. As consumers become wealthier they demand higher-quality, more capital-intensive services

CHAPTER 19
Employment and Unemployment

LEARNING OBJECTIVES

After learning the material in Chapter 19 of *Contemporary Labor Economics*, the student should be able to:

1. explain the various labor force classifications and explain how the Bureau of the Census measures unemployment

2. cite reasons why the official unemployment rate may misrepresent the true extent to which labor is underutilized

3. use stock-flow analysis to describe how changes in labor flows can affect the measured rate of unemployment

4. define and correctly use the term "full employment"

5. use aggregate supply-aggregate demand analysis to show graphically how real output, the price level, and employment are jointly determined

6. distinguish between frictional, structural, and demand-deficient unemployment

7. explain the concept of frictional unemployment and distinguish between "search" unemployment and "wait" unemployment

8. list and analyze the factors which give rise to wait unemployment

9. explain the relative importance of displaced workers as a source of unemployment

10. show graphically how demand-deficient unemployment arises

11. explain why wages adjust slowly in the presence of demand-deficient unemployment

12. describe the current distribution of unemployment across demographic groups

13. describe and analyze the policies which are or may be used to combat unemployment

14. explain the complications which arise in implementing fiscal and monetary policies

15. cite and describe unemployment-reducing alternatives to fiscal and monetary policies

ANSWERS TO SELECTED END-OF-CHAPTER QUESTIONS

1.   a.   Labor force: 220.
       b.   Unemployment rate: 20/220 = 9.09%.
       c.   Labor force participation rate: 220/400 = 55%.

7.   a.   rise   b.   fall   c.   rise

MULTIPLE CHOICE QUESTIONS

1. Which of the following non-working individuals would be considered officially *unemployed* by the Bureau of Labor Statistics?
   a. John, who is beginning a 3-month vacation before reporting to his new job
   b. Ronald, who two months ago gave up his job search in despair because he could not attract a wage offer
   c. Martha, who has not been on the job for the past 4 weeks because she broke her leg
   d.* Hiroshi, who is waiting to be called back to his job from which he was laid off 5 weeks ago

Questions 2 and 3 refer to the following information: The small town of East Macneill has 1,000 residents age 16 or older. During the survey week, 200 adult residents did not work—20 workers were home sick from their jobs, 10 shopkeepers were unable to open their stores due to bad weather, 50 were actively seeking work (25 others had previously given up), and others were either full-time students or home-makers. Of the 800 at work, 80 worked part-time but would have preferred full-time work.

2. The size of labor force in East Macneill is:
   a. 800 persons
   b. 850 persons
   c.* 880 persons
   d. 1,000 persons

3. The official unemployment rate in East Macneill is:
   a. 50/800
   b. 80/800
   c.* 50/880
   d. 50/1,000

Questions 4 and 5 refer to the following information: In Littleville, which has 1,000 residents, 400 people do not currently work. Of these 400 persons, 250 are under age 16, 10 are institutionalized, 15 have become discouraged and quit seeking work, and 75 others are full-time homemakers. Of the 600 who do work, 150 work part-time but wish to work full-time.

4. In Littleville, the number of employed persons is _____ and the size of the labor force is _____.
   a. 600; 1000
   b. 600; 740
   c. 450; 690
   d.* 600; 650

5. What is the official unemployment rate in Littleville?
   a. 400/1000
   b. 50/600
   c.* 50/650
   d. 65/650

6. The official BLS unemployment rate may *overstate* economic hardship because:
   a. all part-time workers are considered fully employed
   b. some workers may be underemployed
   c.* the unemployed include semi-retired workers and teens who wish to work only part-time
   d. the unemployed include people who are not actively seeking work

7. If jobless persons who had given up searching suddenly resumed active searches for paying jobs—but had not yet found any—the unemployment rate would:
   a.* rise
   b. fall
   c. stay the same
   d. more information is needed

Questions 8 – 11 refer to the following diagram:

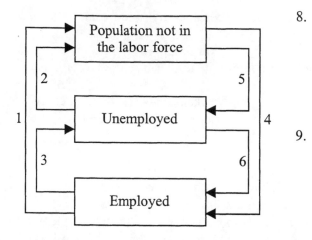

8. An increase in the unemployment rate may be caused by a(n):
    a.* increase in flow 1
    b. increase in flow 2
    c. decrease in flow 5
    d. increase in flow 6

9. Which one of the following would reduce the unemployment rate while leaving the size of the labor force constant?
    a. An increase in flow 1
    b. An increase in flow 2
    c. An increase in flow 3
    d.* An increase in flow 6

10. If flow 4 increases and flows 3 and 5 decrease, then the unemployment rate should:
    a. rise
    b.* fall
    c. stay the same
    d. change, but it cannot be determined how

11. If flow 2 increases, then the unemployment rate will go _____; if flow 6 decreases, then the unemployment rate will go _____.
    a. up; up
    b. up; down
    c.* down; up
    d. down; down

13. The term "natural rate of unemployment" refers to the unemployment rate that will occur:
    a. whenever the actual rate of inflation exceeds the actual rate
    b. if the actual rate of inflation is zero
    c. if the expected rate of inflation is zero
    d.* in the long run if the actual rate of inflation equals the expected rate

14. The unemployment rate at which there is neither excess demand nor excess supply in the aggregate labor market:
    a. must be 0%
    b.* is called the "natural rate of unemployment"
    c. will lead to higher inflation if pursued as a policy goal
    d. corresponds to the rate we would observe if inflation were lower than had been expected

15. One reason the aggregate demand curve slopes downward and to the right is because of a phenomenon known as the "real balance effect." As the price level rises:
    a. the real value of assets rises, which leads people to increase spending on normal goods and services
    b. the real value of assets rises, which leads people to decrease spending on normal goods and services
    c. the real value of assets falls, which leads people to increase spending on normal goods and services
    d.* the real value of assets falls, which leads people to decrease spending on normal goods and services

16. One reason the aggregate demand curve slopes downward and to the right is because of a phenomenon known as the "interest rate effect." As the price level rises:
    a.* more money is demanded, interest rates rise, and investment spending falls
    b. less money is demanded, so consumption spending must fall to maintain equality of investment and savings
    c. the value of assets rises, increasing bank profits and total lending
    d. the Fed raises interest rates, and investment spending rises

17. If a drop in aggregate demand results in an economic recession, then over this range of falling demand the aggregate supply curve is:
    a. vertical   c.* upward sloping
    b. downward sloping   d. inelastic

18. In the short run, the aggregate quantity supplied may exceed the "full-employment" level of output because as the price level rises:
    a. firms mistake lower real wage rates for lower money wage rates and therefore increase employment beyond the profit maximizing level
    b. firms mistake lower money wage rates for lower real wage rates and therefore increase employment beyond the profit maximizing level
    c. workers respond to falling real wage rates by working more hours, since the income effect outweighs the substitution effect
    d.* unemployed workers mistake higher nominal wage rates for higher real wage rates, causing employment and output to rise as they accept job offers more quickly

Questions 19 and 20 refer to the following aggregate demand-aggregate supply diagram:

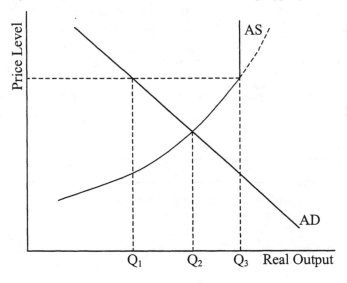

19. The full employment level of output is given by:
    a. Q_1 c.* Q_3
    b. Q_2 d. $Q_3 - Q_1$

20. If aggregate demand is given by AD, the economy will:
    a. achieve the full employment level of output
    b.* fall short of the full employment level of output
    c. exceed the full employment level of output
    d. experience frictional unemployment, but not cyclical unemployment

21. Which of the following is a form of frictional unemployment?
    a.* Wait unemployment   c. Cyclical unemployment
    b. Structural unemployment   d. Displaced workers

22. Which of the following is *not* a source of wait unemployment?
    a. Temporary layoffs   c. Efficiency wages
    b. Union job queues   d.* Changes in the structure of the economy

23. Structural unemployment is characterized by:
    a.* a geographical or skill-based mismatch between available jobs and job seekers
    b. a deficiency in aggregate demand
    c. unemployment in excess of the natural rate
    d. rigidity in wages

24. The type of unemployment commonly associated with displaced workers is:
    a. search unemployment   c.* structural unemployment
    b. wait unemployment   d. demand-deficient unemployment

25. Of the almost 2.5 million workers displaced from their jobs between 1993 and 1994, by January of 1996 most:
    a. were still unemployed
    b. were employed in new jobs, with nearly all workers earning less than before
    c. had dropped out of the labor force
    d.* were employed in new jobs, with about half the workers earning more than before

26. Which one of the following is a *true* statement?
    a. Higher levels of education are associated with higher levels of structural unemployment
    b. During a recession, cyclical unemployment rises but structural unemployment falls
    c.* Historically, technological change has created more jobs than it has made obsolete
    d. The majority of the unemployed during a recession are considered structurally unemployed

27. Demand-deficient unemployment occurs when:
    a. an increase in aggregate supply reduces wage rates, causing fewer people to seek jobs
    b.* a decrease in aggregate demand causes a decrease in the demand for labor, with little reduction in real wage rates
    c. a decrease in aggregate demand causes a decrease in wage rates, causing fewer people to seek jobs
    d. a decrease in aggregate supply reduces consumer demand, thereby reducing the demand for labor

28. Which of the following is *not* a source of downward wage rigidity?
    a. Unions appear to prefer layoffs to wage reductions as the former affects only workers without seniority, while the latter would affect all workers
    b. Firms appear to prefer layoffs to wage reductions as the former allows the firm to "hoard" workers in whom they have invested specific training
    c. Implicit contracts
    d.* Layoffs are discouraged due to the method used to finance unemployment compensation insurance

29. Wages may be inflexible downward during a period of cyclical unemployment because:
    a. insiders may fear harassment from outsiders who "stole" their jobs
    b.* outsiders may fear harassment from insiders and are thus unwilling to work for lower wages
    c. firms believe that outsiders will withhold cooperation from insiders who "stole" their jobs
    d. both insiders and outsiders will withhold cooperation from management if management reduces wages

30. Implicit contracts imply that:
   a. firms may lay off workers in return for granting them an "insurance policy" against wage reductions
   b.* firms may pay workers a lower wage in return for granting them an "insurance policy" against layoff
   c. firms have a higher wage bill in recessions than during periods of economic expansion
   d. firms have an incentive to contract with workers to pay them the going market wage

31. Which one of the following is a *true* statement?
   a. Unemployment rates are greater for occupations requiring greater amounts of human capital
   b.* Historically, the black unemployment rate has been about twice that for whites
   c. The proportion of the unemployed who have been looking for jobs for an extended period (15 weeks or more) falls during a recession
   d. Historically, the unemployment rate for females has been twice that of males

32. _____ of the unemployment rate differential between black and white men can be explained by characteristics like education and job experience, which suggests that discrimination plays _____ in the unemployment gap.
   a. Nearly all; little or no role   c. Nearly all; a role
   b.* Less than half; a role   d. Less than half; little or no role

33. An increase in government demand for output is a tool that would most likely be used to combat:
   a. search unemployment   c. structural unemployment
   b. wait unemployment   d.* demand-deficient unemployment

34. The purpose of a Keynesian fiscal policy to combat demand-deficient unemployment in a recession is to:
   a.* increase aggregate demand so that it intersects aggregate supply at the full employment level of output
   b. decrease aggregate demand so that it intersects aggregate supply at the full employment level of output
   c. increase the money supply by a constant 4% annual rate
   d. decrease aggregate supply such that it intersects aggregate demand at the full employment level of output

35. "Crowding out" occurs when:
   a. unemployment rises as a result of downward wage rigidity
   b. unemployment rises because workers are displaced
   c.* government borrowing pushes up interest rates, causing private investment to fall
   d. government borrowing pushes up interest rates, thereby leading fiscal policy to overshoot the expansion of aggregate demand

36. Suppose that a policy response to cyclical unemployment is mistimed or overshoots its target, thereby resulting in output *above* the full employment level. Output will:
   a.* eventually return to the full employment level because workers will no longer supply as much labor at each nominal wage
   b. eventually return to the full employment level because nominal wage rates are rigid
   c. eventually return to the full employment level because workers will not adjust their acceptance wages
   d. stay above the full employment level

37.   (*World of Work* 19-1) A study by Ruhm on the effects of the Worker Adjustment and Retraining Notification (WARN) Act of 1988 suggests that:
    a.*   prenotification of plant closings has resulted in a slight reduction of the average unemployment spell
    b.   prenotification of plant closings has actually resulted in longer unemployment spells
    c.   prenotification of plant closings has actually resulted in higher unemployment rates
    d.   almost all employers which closed plants have complied with the law

38.   (*World of Work* 19-2) The theoretical advantage of Weitzman's "Share Economy" is that:
    a.*   wages would automatically fall in a recession, thereby reducing the impact on employment of a decline in aggregate demand
    b.   employers will be encouraged to use relatively more capital, which will raise productivity
    c.   workers prefer greater employment stability to earnings stability
    d.   workers would gain a tax advantage, as wage earnings are currently taxed at higher rates than share earnings

SAMPLE PROBLEMS AND ESSAY QUESTIONS

1. On a diagram, draw a typical individual's labor supply curve. On a separate diagram, draw a typical market labor supply curve. Reconcile any differences.

2. On a labor leisure-choice diagram, illustrate the impact on desired hours of work resulting from an increase in non-wage income. Assume leisure is a normal good.

3. Use the diagram below to answer the following questions.

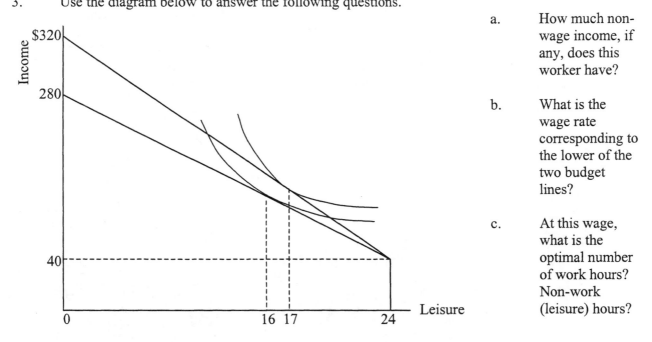

a. How much non-wage income, if any, does this worker have?

b. What is the wage rate corresponding to the lower of the two budget lines?

c. At this wage, what is the optimal number of work hours? Non-work (leisure) hours?

d. Suppose the wage rises as shown by the upper budget line. Is this person on the upward sloping or backward-bending portion of her labor supply curve?

e. On the diagram, decompose the change in observed work hours resulting from the wage change into its component income and substitution effects. Which effect dominates?

4. For each group identified in bold type below, use the labor-leisure choice model to illustrate graphically and then explain the change in the quantity of leisure consumed. Be sure to explain how the group's labor force participation rate is affected.
    a. The earnings of married men have decreased, thereby reducing the nonwage incomes of **married women**.
    b. Real wage rates for **women** have increased. Further, the substitution effect for women is stronger than the income effect.
    c. Real wage rates for **men** have increased. Further, the substitution effect for men is dominated by the income effect.
    d. **Married women** exhibit a stronger preference for market work over other nonmarket uses of time.
    e. Social Security has increased benefits and widened coverage for **older citizens**.

5.   Consider a typical family consisting of two (market) working parents and their two children. One of the spouses is then given a substantial raise. Speculate how this family's allocation of time might change, explaining the reasons for any changes you identify. As part of your answer, define the terms "income effect" and "substitution effect."

6.   Suppose tax laws are changed such that households with children receive a lump sum tax credit on earned income below $25,000. Use the labor-leisure choice model to illustrate graphically and then explain the change in the quantity of labor supplied by households with children:
a.   earning $25,000 or less
b.   earning more than $25,000

7.   Many colleges and universities are not too concerned about student enrollments when the economy enters a recession. In fact, college enrollment tends to be countercyclical. Use a model of human capital to suggest why this might be the case.

8.   Use Becker's supply and demand model of human capital below to show and explain why an increase in the college wage premium should increase the numbers of individuals who attend college.

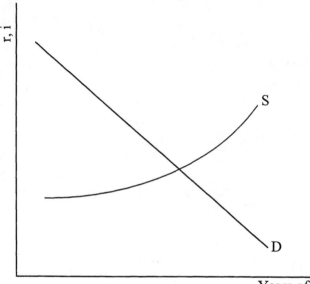

Years of schooling

9.   a.   Why does investment in on-the-job training diminish with age?
         b.   Predict the effect of each of the following on the probability of college attendance. Explain your answers.
              i.   The direct costs of college rise.
              ii.   The gap between earnings of college and high-school graduates widens.
              iii.   The rate of discount decreases.

10. Consider the following information.

Employees	Output	Price
0	0	$5.00
1	10	5.00
2	25	5.00
3	35	5.00
4	40	5.00
5	43	5.00
6	44	5.00
7	44	5.00

a. Does this firm have monopoly power? How do you know?
b. How many workers would the firm hire if the wage were $65? $45? $20? $8?

11. Consider the following information.

Employees	Output	Price
0	0	$5.00
1	20	4.50
2	50	4.00
3	75	3.50
4	95	3.00
5	110	2.50
6	120	2.00
7	125	1.50
8	125	1.50

a. Construct a short-run labor demand curve from the following production and product demand data.
b. In what sense will the long-run demand curve differ from the short-run curve derived in part a.?

12. The following diagram shows a competitive labor market and an individual firm hiring in the market. On the graphs, indicate:
   a. the equilibrium wage
   b. the firm's demand for labor curve
   c. the firm's equilibrium employment
   d. the total payment to labor in the firm
   e. the total return to capital in the firm

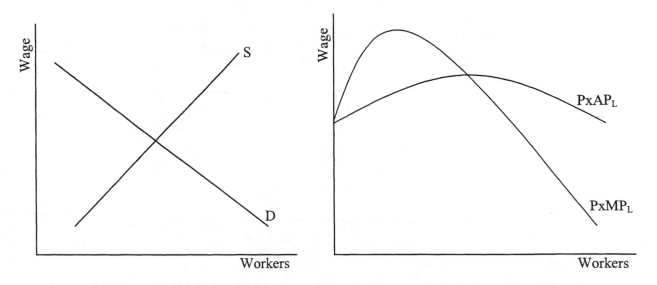

13. State three of the four Hicks-Marshall laws of derived demand ("The demand for labor is more elastic ...."). For any one of these, give as detailed an explanation as you can of why it is true.

14. The Boeing Aircraft Company currently employs upwards of 80,000 employees in the Puget Sound region, and hires a huge proportion of the available supply of aeronautical engineers.
    a. On the diagram below, illustrate the wage and employment level of aeronautical engineers in the region, assuming Boeing exploits its monopsony position and assuming no unions. Label W_m and L_m.
    b. Alter your diagram to incorporate the fact that most engineers belong to SPEA, the engineering union, which negotiates with Boeing over wages. Label the wage and employment W_u and L_u, respectively.
    c. Does the union likely improve or worsen any labor misallocations? Explain briefly.

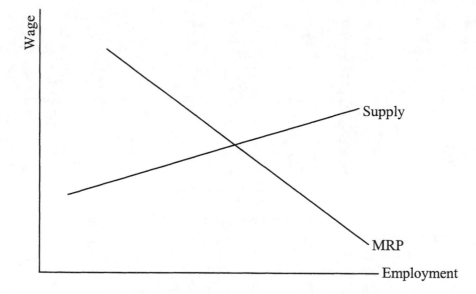

15. Explain what is meant when an economist says that competitive labor markets are "efficient." Are labor markets efficient if a firm has monopsony power? Explain and graph.

16. Both monopolies which hire from competitive labor markets and monopsonies which sell output in competitive markets tend to hire less than the socially optimal level of employees. Use the diagrams below to illustrate. Indicate on the diagrams the actual levels of employment and the optimal levels of employment.

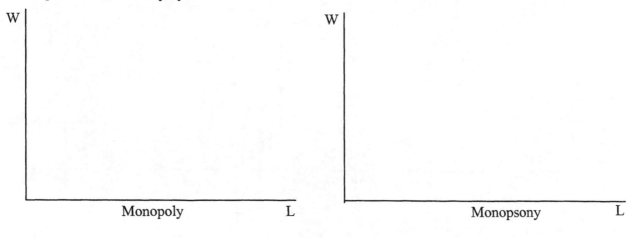

164

17. Cite four methods by which firms may structure their pay systems to improve worker productivity. For each of these methods, cite its potential drawbacks.

18. Define the term "economic efficiency" as it relates to labor markets. Under what conditions will it be achieved? How must this definition be altered to account for differences in pay schemes across different industries and firms?

19. a. On the diagram below, illustrate the work/leisure choice facing a *salaried* employee.

b. Using indifference curves, illustrate on the graph the utility-maximizing choice of hours worked (assuming no monitoring).

c. How do you reconcile your answer to part b. with the observation that, on average, salaried employees work longer hours than hourly employees?

Income

Hours/day

20. Explain the concept "principal-agent problem" as it arises in the labor market. Describe two methods by which the firm may structure pay so as to reduce or eliminate this problem, citing the strengths and weaknesses of each.

21. Assume that on average, men and women have different preferences regarding the work environment. Suppose, for example, that while both women and men prefer being around other people to working solitary, the average woman prefers—more than the average man—working collaboratively and being in what is usually called a "people" job. Further suppose that different firms have different costs of providing these work conditions: some jobs, like real-estate sales, are naturally of this type, while others, such as factory work, are of a more solitary nature. Use a hedonic model to examine pay for the average man versus pay for the average woman, all else equal. Does the model have anything to say about whether men are any better off (have higher utility) than women?

22. What is the theory of compensating wage differentials? Explain. Suppose workers with similar skills and education earn different wages. Cite and discuss five circumstances under which these wage differentials will persist.

23. Suppose Occupation A requires a bachelor's degree. Suppose Occupation B requires a bachelor's degree and five years of post-schooling training.
    a. Other things equal, which occupation will tend to pay higher wages? Explain.
    b. Under what circumstances will occupation A pay a higher wage than B? Discuss.

24. a. Of what relevance are information and costs of mobility in the hedonic theory of wages? Explain and illustrate with appropriate graphical analysis.
    b. If information is imperfect, then how are wage differentials affected? Explain and graph.
    c. If mobility is costly, then how are wage differentials affected? Explain and graph.

25. Explain carefully: "If all workers and jobs were identical, there would be just one wage rate, assuming perfect information and costless mobility." As part of your answer, use the graphs below to illustrate what would happen if wages were initially unequal. Be sure to explain the role of the two assumptions given—what happens if they are violated?

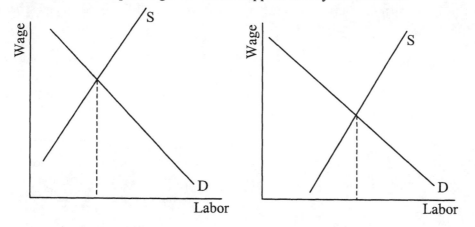

26. Describe how migration can be interpreted as an investment in human capital. What circumstances *increase* the likelihood that a person will migrate to another work location? Explain, presenting examples.

27. In a famous 1941 paper, Wolfgang Stolper and Paul Samuelson showed that a decline in U.S. tariffs on imported goods would reduce U.S. wages relative to the rest of the world. (This result hinges on the fact that capital is abundant in the U.S. relative to our trading partners.) NAFTA, the North American Free Trade Agreement, reduced tariffs substantially between the U.S. and Mexico. If Stolper and Samuelson were correct, predict the effect of NAFTA on immigration into the U.S. from Mexico. Explain briefly how international trading of goods and services, or international capital movements, reinforce the economic impacts of international migration.

28. Is the following statement true, false, or uncertain? "If we deported all illegal aliens who are now in the United States, our total national unemployment would decline by the same number of people." Explain carefully; use the graph at right to support your answer.

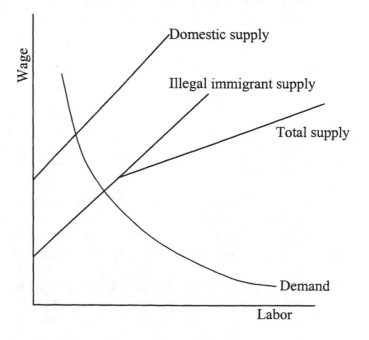

166

29.   a.   Why are there "real negative externalities" associated with migration?
      b.   Discuss the various "pecuniary externalities" associated with migration.

30.   Briefly describe the characteristics of the "typical" union member with respect to gender, race, geographical location, education, and occupation. How might changes in these characteristics explain the relative decline in union membership? Discuss two other explanations for this decline.

31.   Discuss in detail the various difficulties of accurately measuring the union-nonunion wage differential.

32.   Three examples of union bargaining tactics are a) voting overwhelmingly to authorize a strike, b) placing a full-page ad in the local paper outlining the reasonableness of its position, and c) reducing its wage demand by $.25 per hour. For each, explain the impact of the tactic on the bargaining power of the union, indicating whether the tactic is persuasive or coercive.

33.   Evaluate the following claim using the diagram below: "Unions cause an inefficient allocation of labor, since too few workers end up in union jobs."

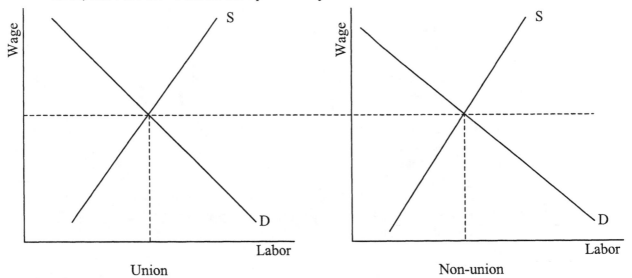

Union   Non-union

34.   How is labor supply affected by the existence of public goods? Give two examples.

35.   What is the economic incidence of the payroll tax—that is, who really "pays" the taxes for Medicare, Social Security, and Disability Insurance? Use a graph to illustrate your answer.

36.   Explain the main features of the following acts of labor legislation. Discuss how each act affected union bargaining power.
      a.   Wagner Act
      b.   Taft-Hartley Act

37.   Explain, using specific examples, how changes in the U.S. legal system have led to changes—both increases and decreases—in the extent of (a) unionism, and (b) labor market discrimination.

38. Explain how an increase in the minimum wage will affect employment in (a) a labor market where the wage rate is below the new minimum wage, and (b) a labor market where the wage rate already exceeds the new minimum wage.

39. Explain how an increase in minimum safety standards will affect the wage rate in (a) a sector where job safety is below the new minimum standard, and (b) a sector where job safety already exceeds the new safety standard.

40. Under what conditions will a minimum wage reduce employment? Under what conditions, if any, might a minimum wage increase employment? Use (labeled!) graphs as part of your answer, and explain carefully.

41. Any ship entering Puget Sound (a large bay in the Pacific Northwest) is required to have a state-certified "pilot" aboard to guide the ship safely to port. On a supply and demand diagram for Sound pilots, illustrate the impacts of this requirement in terms of economic rent. Who likely argued that this requirement was necessary—the state? Pilots? Consumers? Owners of shipping companies? Explain.

42. A firm's costs and benefits of providing safety on the job are shown in the diagram at right.
    a. What are the benefits of providing safety? The costs?
    b. Show how much safety this firm will provide.
    c. Is this the "right" amount? Explain.
    d. Suppose workers discover that this job is actually more risky than they previously believed. Illustrate this on the diagram and predict what will happen to the amount of actual safety on this job in the future.

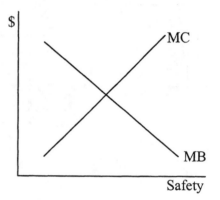

43. Explain the main features of the following acts of labor legislation. Discuss how each act affected labor market discrimination.
    a. Equal Pay Act
    b. Civil Rights Act

44. Discuss: "It is in the employer's best interest to separate productivity differences from other worker characteristics such as race and gender. Discrimination is costly." Is discrimination costly? If so, what labor market outcomes can be predicted for firms which discriminate? Under what circumstances, if any, is the statement false?

45. Briefly explain the "market-power" (monopsony) model of discrimination as it applies to male/female wages. What market condition is required to get the result that men receive higher wages than women? Do you think such a condition squares with reality? Explain briefly.

46. Explain briefly what is meant by the term "statistical discrimination." Give an example.

47. According to Milton Friedman and Thomas Sowell, labor market discrimination cannot persist. Summarize the arguments of these free-market economists.

48. The following diagram reflects occupational crowding of women. Imagine that occupational discrimination were suddenly eliminated and women were free to enter any occupation. Illustrate the effects on the diagram, and show what impact this has on allocative efficiency. Explain your answers.

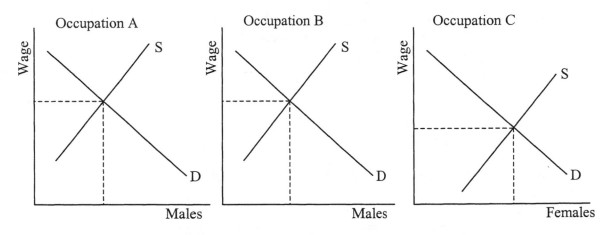

49. In recent years, the federal government has introduced and then expanded a law which subjects some unemployment benefits to the income tax. Use a job search model to discuss the likely impacts of this law on (a) job search duration, (b) the unemployment rate, and (c) economic efficiency.

50. What are the advantages to workers of internal labor markets? Are there advantages to firms? Do internal labor markets necessarily improve economic efficiency? Explain.

51. Sketch a hypothetical earnings distribution and its corresponding Lorenz curve. For each illustration, show how the diagram would change should earnings inequality increase.

52. To what extent are observed differences in earnings the result of rational choices? What other factors might account for these differences?

53. Consider the following annual earnings data:
    Lowest 1/5   5%
    Second 1/5   8%
    Middle 1/5   17%
    Fourth 1/5   25%
    Top 1/5   45%

    a.   Plot these data as a Lorenz curve. Show your intermediate calculations.
    b.   Shade in the area which roughly corresponds to the Gini ratio.
    c.   Sketch a Lorenz curve which might correspond to *lifetime* earnings in this economy.

54. Will tax changes to redistribute income from higher-income to lower-income persons necessarily affect the Gini coefficient? Explain why or why not. Define the term "Gini coefficient" as part of your answer.

55. What is the relationship between money wage increases, productivity increases, and product price increases?

56.   a.   What elasticity conditions are least helpful for long-run employment growth in an
           industry? Explain.
      b.   Is the following statement accurate? Explain why or why not. "Employment growth is
           greatest in those industries in which productivity growth is greatest."

57.   Consider the three labor force states one may be in: Employed (E), unemployed (U), or not in the
      labor force (N). What is the impact on the unemployment rate of each of the following?
      a.   An increase in the rate of flow of people from N to U
      b.   An increase in the rate of flow of people from U to N
      c.   An increase in the rate of flow of people from U to E
      d.   An increase in the rate of flow of people from E to N
      e.   Which of the above best corresponds to the notion of "discouraged workers"?
      f.   Which of the above best corresponds to an increase in people taking early retirement?

58.   Explain the differences between structural unemployment, cyclical unemployment, and frictional
      unemployment.

59.   a.   Discuss four separate reasons why wages may be inflexible downward.
      b.   Explain how wage rigidity might contribute to unemployment.
      c.   Analyze how wage rigidity might affect productivity over the business cycle.